Reprint of 1918 edition

Series editors: Peter Mittenthal and Marianne Stenbaek
Cover photograph courtesy NASA, Visible Earth
Distributed by University Press of New England
www.upne.com

ISBN 978-0-9821703-4-2

International Polar Institute Press
P.O. Box 212, Hanover, NH 03755 USA
&
McGill University/Arts Building
853 Sherbrooke St. West, Montreal, PQ H3A 2T6 Canada

www.ipolari.com

TALES OF YUKAGHIR

LAMUT, AND RUSSIANIZED NATIVES OF EASTERN SIBERIA

by

WALDEMAR BOGORAS

IPI Press

Distributed by University Press of New England
London and Hanover

INTRODUCTION from original edition

The following tales were collected among Russianized natives of the Kolyma and the Anadyr country, and also among Russian Creoles, who, indeed, lead the same kind of life as the Russianized natives. I have excluded a large number of those tales which treat of kings, young heroes on horseback, etc., and which, on the whole, clearly show their Russian or Turko-Mongol provenience, and have given only those that represent elements of native life. The narrators ascribe quite a number of the tales given here to the Lamut, Yukaghir, or Chuvantzi; but, so far as I am able to judge, most of those coming from the Kolyma indicate a Yukaghir provenience, and those from the Anadyr would seem to be of Chuvantzi origin. Nothing more definite than this is known. Most of the tales were taken down by myself, a large part by Mrs. Sophie Bogoras, and a few by a couple of Russian Creoles who could read and write after a fashion.

The majority have titles corresponding to their context, which must be due to Russian influence, as the same stories in native languages barely have titles.

As to the transcription of proper names and such words as are said to belong to native languages, I have used, for the more or less Russianized words, the usual English alphabet; and for native words not Russianized, the special alphabet which I have used in the Publications of the Jesup North Pacific Expedition, vol. 1.

Some of the tales are composed in part of rhymed prose. Some of these prose rhymes, though quite local and native as to contents, are arranged in the form of the ancient Russian lays. For most of these I give the Russian text with English translation. Notes signed W. B. are by the author. A few comparative notes have been added by Franz Boas and signed with his initials.

Waldemar Bogoras

CONTENTS

III. KOLYMA TALES

INTRODUCTION

Tales of Yukaghir, Lamut and Russianized Natives of Eastern Siberia were collected from the end of the 19th to the early 20th centuries by Waldemar Bogoras and his wife Sophie in the Anadyr and Kolyma regions. The stories were told by a number of different indigenous peoples living in these areas—not just Yukaghir and Lamut (as they were called then, now referred to as Even) mentioned in the title. The "Russianized" natives include Chuvantzy. The collection was first published in 1918 in the series of Anthropological Papers (volume XX, Part I) of the American Museum of Natural History. The books in this series by Bogoras and his close friend and colleague Waldemar Jochelson provide the best accounts we have of the people living in this part of Siberia at this time in history.

Waldemar Bogoras, as he is known in English, was born in Western Ukraine in 1865. He was named Natan (in English, Nathan) by his parents, which he changed to Vladimir in 1885 when he adopted the Orthodox Church. At that time he took on the patronymic Germanovich after his godfather. Bogoras used the pseudonym N. A. Tan, based on his given first name, for his belletristic writings and is often known in Russian as Bogoraz-Tan or Tan-Bogoraz. He is well-known to this day in Russia as a prime figure in the establishment of Russian ethnography, and as the founder of the Institute of the Northern Peoples in Leningrad.

The majority of the tales in this volume were collected by Bogoras himself in the period 1895-1896. A few tales were collected later, in 1900, and some of those were recorded by his wife Sophie. The different dates in fact represent two different periods of stay in Siberia, a fact which we know from the historical records but is not mentioned by Bogoras himself. The first "trip" to the Kolyma and Anadyr regions was in fact one of political exile: Bogoras was sent to the Kolyma region in May 1889 for ten years for anti-tsarist activities in his affiliation with the revolutionary group Narodnaya Volya ('People's Will'). From the time of his arrival in Kolyma in 1890 until 1896 he spent his time studying the local (Russian) speech patterns and enthusiastically collecting Russian material—folktales, riddles, songs and proverbs. After he exhausted his study of the local Russian folklore and language, his interests turned to the neighboring indigenous people, the Chukchee. Bogoras became frustrated by local interpreters who clearly had no better command of the Chukchee language than he did, and set about learning it thoroughly. During this period he came to understand the importance of language as a key to understanding any culture, and in his own writings argues that language is "the best means for getting to know the people themselves, a means which is flawless and exact" (Bogoraz 1930:85) and, moreover, that language was the only means to truly understand the full depth of a people and their culture. His understanding of the intimate connections between language and culture, and of the means for an outsider to study them, is all the more remarkable given that Bogoras had had no formal training in ethnography or linguistics prior to his exile. In fact, he became one of the founding fathers of Soviet/Russian ethnography through his firsthand experiences in Siberia.

In November 1898 the ten-year exile was over and Bogoras returned to St. Petersburg. His second trip to Siberia took place in conjunction with the Jesup North Pacific Expedition, which ran from 1897-1902 and was personally funded by Morris Jesup, who was president of the American Museum of Natural History at the time. The expedition was actually conceived of and directed by the American anthropologist Franz Boas, and it was Boas who first contacted Waldemar Jochelson to ask him to oversee the Siberian part of the expedition. Upon Jochelson's recommendation, Bogoras was also invited to take part in the expedition, with the understanding that Bogoras would be responsible for the study of the Chukchee people, with whom he had spent extensive time during his exile to Siberia. He proposed to Boas that his part of the expedition begin in the village of Markovo, Anadyr region. A number of the stories in the Tales were collected at this time, specifically those in Parts V, Markovo Tales, and Part VI, Anadyr Tales, as well as a few in other sections of the book. Many of the Markovo and Anadyr tales were recorded by Sophie Bogoras, who accompanied her husband on this expedition. The findings of this extensive expedition were published as a special series entitled Publications of the Jesup North Pacific Expedition, first by the American Museum of Natural History in New York (1898-1903) and then by E.J. Brill in Leiden and G.E. Stechert in New York (1905-1930). This series includes Jochelson's own significant contributions to our understandings of the peoples of this region, among which is his 1926 study of the Yukaghir and the Yukaghirized Tungus (volume IX, parts I-III). And Bogoras's own publications are the authoritative ethnographic sources for the Chukchee to this day. These include his books on The Chukchee and Chukchee Mythology, published in the Jesup

North Pacific Expedition as Volume 7 (1904-1920) and Volume 9, part 1 (1910), respectively.

Bogoras's own introduction to the Tales is brief and provides some rather incomplete information about the stories themselves. He himself transcribed the majority of the Tales, although some were written down by his wife Sophie, and a few, he notes, were transcribed by Russian creoles. Detailed ethnographic information is lacking, although it should be noted that Bogoras was meticulous in recording what today would be called core metadata—the date and place of each recording and the name of each speaker. There is also little indication of exactly what his descriptions of the narrators mean. For example, one is described as "Russianized Chuvantsi woman," another as a "Russianized Yukaghir," but it is unclear if that means that the speakers self-identified as Chuvantsi or Yukaghir but spoke only Russian, or were bilingual, or what. Several are described as "Russian creoles" but again, it is not stated how that determination was made or what it is intended to convey. The modern ethnographer or linguist, however, would prefer to know more details about individual speakers, such as age, languages spoken in the home, clan affiliation, information about parents and their languages and clan affiliation. This is in part a reflection of the time, in part a reflection of Bogoras's own lack of formal training in ethnography and, perhaps even more importantly, a reflection of the peoples' own understanding of their identity. The larger sense of tribal affiliation was more a Soviet construct in the government's attempt to build nations and "nationalities," than an ingrained sense of identity. In pre-Soviet times, identity was only loosely understood along tribal lines, with clan affiliation and places taking precedent. This loose understanding of ethnicity accounts for the discrepancy between what the narrators told Bogoras about the tales (as being specifically Even, Yukaghir or Chuvantzi in origin), as opposed to his own estimation that those from Kolyma are essentially Yukaghir, while those of Anadyr essentially Chuvantzi. In some of the stories, the narrator explains that he or she is uncertain if the main character is Yakut or Yukaghir, or "something else." Notable in this regard is the La'la tale: in the Kolyma version, the Chuvantzi hero La'la and his brother are referred to as Yukaghir, while in the Anadyr version, La'la is clearly Chuvantzy. While some of these discrepancies may be due to attrition of the language and culture, accompanied by a general loss of the details of the folklore, they also underscore the rather fluid sense of identity among the indigenous peoples of the time.

It should also be noted that it is unclear from reading the notes to the Tales as to what criteria Bogoras himself used in determining ethnicity. Language is one obvious factor, but is problematic for the Russianized segment of the population, and because so many of the people were bi- or multi-lingual at the time, at least to some degree.

The Peoples of the Kolyma and Anadyr Regions

Bogoras mentions several different ethnic groups: the Yukaghirs, the Lamut, the Tungus, the Chuvantzi and the Creoles. Just how to determine the ethnic identity of these people is complicated in general, and further complicated by the fact that they are "Russianized," to use Bogoras's term. Part of the difficulty comes from naming issues, as some of these have changed. The "Lamut" are referred to as Even today, and the "Tungus" as Evenki. They are closely related ethnolinguistically, both languages being part of the Tungusic language family, a group of languages spoken over a vast range of Siberia and into China. Manchu is probably the most famous of the Tungusic languages, but the Even and Evenki are quite distant relatives of the Manchu.

Judging by reports from Bogoras himself, the lingua franca of the region at the time was Chukchee, a Paleo-Siberian language representing yet another, quite different ethnolinguistic Siberian people. He notes that Chuvantzi, Evenki and Yukaghir all had a certain command of Chukchee. The Chukchee were nomadic reindeer herders and enjoyed the greatest prosperity of any group for at least two hundred years, roaming throughout the Kolyma region with their herds as far as the Bering Strait. In their travels, they thus came in contact with the various groups living throughout the area—ranging from the Yupiks in the east, the Yukaghirs, Evens (Lamuts), Evenki (Tungus) and Sakha (Yakuts) in the west. Today, it should be noted, Chukchee is highly endangered. It has been replaced as a lingua franca for the region by Russian and by Sakha (Yakut). Sakha is a Turkic language which was probably already overtaking Chukchee in terms of dominance when Bogoras arrived.

In addition, the Siberian indigenous peoples of the time did not have a strong sense of ethnic identity in the modern sense. Identity was more fluid and ran along linguistic and clan lines more than ethnic blood lines.

Yukaghir

In the 17th century the Yukaghir tribes roamed a vast territory of Siberia from the delta of the Lena river to the Anadyr. The Yukaghir languages are not clearly related to any other language spoken today (although the now extinct language spoken by the Chuvantzi was probably related). Yukaghir is spoken in two different varieties today; historically these were considered dialects of one language but today are seen as separate languages because they are so different. Both are highly endangered today, with a total of only about 240 speakers as of the 2002 census. The language spoken in Kolyma, along the Kolyma River, is Southern, or Kolyma Yukaghir. It is not mutually intelligible with Northern, or Tundra Yukaghir, which is spoken in Sakha (Yakutia) and Kamchatka. Even at the time of colonization, the two were so different that the different groups did not necessarily see that they were related to one another. This was compounded by the lack of a self-ethnonym or greater sense of ethnic identity. Although Russians knew them all as Yukaghirs, they themselves lacked a common ethnonyms for their united tribe and referred to themselves either by local names or by the term odul – 'strong', 'powerful'. The term Yukaghir may have been given to them by the Evenki (Tungus), as the suffix -ghir (or -gir) is often found in Tungusic clan names.

The Yukaghir of the time of Bogoras were most thoroughly studied by Jochelson who spent the years 1895-1896 studying them, returning in 1900 as part of the Jessup Expedition. Jochelson notes that the tribe is "dying out" and writes of strong assimilation of the Yukaghirs to the Evenki (Tungus). Available census information confirms this: in 1640 there were an estimated 4500-5000 people, while the census of 1897 lists only 948 people. These numbers need to be taken with caution as the lack of a broad sense of ethnic identity among Yukaghirs at the time must surely have had some impact on the assessment of population size. But Jochelson's own experiences confirm the general trend in the numbers, and the stories which appear here in the Tales, again, come from those Yukaghirs who are already Russianized. This Russification certainly had begun long before Bogoras arrived in Kolyma.

Chuvantzi

The Chuvantzi are first mentioned in the middle of the 17th century in Russian sources as a group of people belonging to a Yukaghir clan. They were the first native peoples in the region who were required to pay tribute during the period of Russian colonization of Siberia and so came to serve as intermediaries between the Russians and other indigenous groups, a fact which may have contributed to their relatively early assimilation. In the 18th century they traveled with their herds, hunted and fished, along the Anadyr river and its branches but in the 18th century, under pressure from the Chukchee, they were pushed into the Kolyma region where they became Russified. Their language was related to Yukaghir and is reported to have been completely extinct by the late 19th century. By the middle of the 19th century two groups of Chuvantzi had emerged: the "Markovtsy," Chuvantzi who lived in the area of the village of Markovo and were settled, while the second group, those living in the Anadyr region, were nomadic, herders and hunters, living the traditional lifestyle of the neighboring Chukchee and Koryaks, and assimilated to them. According to the 1897 census, there were a total of 452 Chuvantzi, with 275 of them settled and the remaining 177 nomadic. Subsequent Soviet censuses did not recognize them as a distinct group until 1989; before that they were counted either as Russians, or as Chukchee. The speakers whom Bogoras refers to as "Russianized Chuvantzi" almost certainly were. The Chuvantzi spoke a variety of Russian based on local, regional dialect of the Russian settlers of the 17th and 18th centuries, with a relatively large number of borrowings from the languages they were in contact with—Yukaghir, Even (Lamut), Chukchee and Sakha (Yakut). To this day, the Chuvantzi have a strong sense of identity and see themselves as different from the other groups in the region, despite their loss of language centuries ago, and see themselves as speaking a language which is quite distinct from Russian.

The Tungusic Peoples, "Lamut" (Even) and "Tungus" (Evenki)

The term Lamut was used by Russians during the time of Bogoras to refer to a group of Tungusic people who now refer to themselves as Even, while Tungus was used for present-day Evenki. Although their modern names are similar, these are clearly distinct languages and both have many dialects which are not always mutually intelligible. The Evens are smaller in number than the Evenki and historically have lived further to the north and to the northeast than the Evenki, pushed there from the 17th century as Russians colonized the more southern and western areas. This continues to be the case to this day. At present they live in rather dispersed groups in northeast Siberia, throughout much of present-day Sakha (Yakutia) with clusters living in the upper and middle Kolyma regions. According to the 1989 census, there were 1336 Evens in Chukotka, primarily in Biblino and Anadyr regions, two-thirds of these live in three settlements: Omolon, Aniuisk and Vaegi. A small but permanent Even community lives in Markovo. Traditionally a group of hunters, fishers and reindeer herders, both the Evens and Evenkis experienced in the 1940s-1950 a strong Russian/Soviet influence which seriously affected their language, as did the other minorities of Kolyma. When Bogoras arrived in Kolyma in the late 19th century, the Even were one of the main groups living in the region.

The Even figure large in the Tales, both as narrators and as protagonists in a number of the stories. Their position in these stories suggests the role they played in society at the time, as protagonists are sometimes mistakenly referred to as "the Lamut," a label which Bogoras corrects in a footnote. Or there is the case of the child narrator Kitty, called "the Lamut girl," whom Bogoras identifies as a Russian creole, a curious fact which suggests that the mixed ethnicity may have been a greater factor in identity for Bogoras than for the community in which he found himself.

The Tales of Yukaghir, Lamut and Russianized Natives

More than a collection of purely fictitious folklore, the Tales provide an invaluable wealth of information about the peoples living in the Kolyma and Anadyr regions at the turn of the century, presenting insights into their daily life, their beliefs, trials and triumphs. The Tales tell us of the life of the people in two different ways. First are Bogoras's own notes to the texts, embedded as footnotes. Some stories have no notes from Bogoras, but many do, and these provide important not only meta-commentary about the texts themselves but also information that goes beyond a particular story to the much wider cultural context in which they were embedded. This includes important ethnographic and demographic data, such as Bogoras's discussion of the 30-40 Even families living a Chukchee-like lifestyle in the Chaun region or his extensive note on housing types of different peoples, i.e. the houses of Kamchadal and Koryaks with two entrances, or the tents covered with reindeer-skins which are used by Evenki. Interwoven in the folklore are details of everyday life, ranging from details about the kinds of housing, or interesting cultural details, such as the fact that the certain female characters wear breeches, to which Bogoras adds that breeches are commonly worn by other indigenous women (e.g. Chukchee and Even). The Tales include a wealth of folk explanations for a range of problems that people encountered, such as bad merchants, the spread of epidemic disease (explained by the small pox stories), or stories which are reminiscent of Aesop's Fables in explaining the natural world, tales of why bears sleep in the winter, or in having some moral implicitly embedded in them. Many of the stories are mythical in nature. Common to much of Siberian folklore, characters are often shape-shifting, changing from human to animal form, or the opposite. Supernatural beings—evil witches, powerful shamans and spirits—figure large in many of the stories.

Bogoras deliberately excluded tales of kings or heroes on horseback which he ascribes to Russian or Turko-Mongolic influence, a decision which has clearly affected the content of the volume. Thus the range of stories which Bogoras collected was surely greater, and the Tales must be understood to be an edited selection, rather than a complete and unbiased documentation. In other words, he made a deliberate and conscious decision about what constituted an "authentic" native tale and what was corrupted by borrowing or influence from another culture. At the same time, Bogoras notes parallels between individual stories and similar stories found among other Siberian groups (e.g. Koryak), or sees versions of Russian tales (as in the case of the Kolyma story of the stepmother and the stepdaughter). Significantly, he draws ties to some of the stories with those of Native North America, an intellectual goal which was part of the Jesup Expedition as a whole.

The Tales present a remarkable snapshot of the life and culture of a Siberia which has been lost forever. Strikingly, they capture that moment when many of the peoples were in transition away from a more traditional, indigenous lifestyle to a more Russified lifestyle. Recorded just years before the upheaval of the Bolshevik Revolution and all the changes that it brought to the indigenous peoples of Siberia, they provide an invaluable record for all who wish to know more about that pre-Soviet period, the period before the Far East was thoroughly, irreversibly colonized.

Lenore Grenoble
Dartmouth College

Further reading:

Bogoras, Waldemar. 1904-1909. The Chukchee. Memoirs of the American Museum of Natural History, Volume 11. Leiden, E.J. Brill Ltd.; New York, G.E. Stechert.

Bogoraz, V. G. 1930. L.Ja. Shternberg kak fol'klorist. Sbornik pamjati L.Ja. Shternberg. Leningrad: Uchpedgiz.

Forsyth, James. 1992. A History of the Peoples of Siberia. Russia's North Asian Colony 1581-1990. Cambridge: Cambridge University Press.

Jochelson, Waldemar. 1926. The Yukaghir and the Yukaghirized Tungus. Memoirs of the American Museum of Natural History. [vol. XIII, pt. I-III] Publications of the Jesup North Pacific Expedition. vol. IX, pt. I-III. Leiden: E. J. Brill and New York: G. E. Stechert.

I
TALES OF THE TUNDRA YUKAGHIR[1]

1. (The Girl and the Evil-Spirit.)

There lived a girl who knew no man. Nor could she tell who were her parents. She was rich in reindeer and other property. So she walked about, singing lustily. She never went to watch over her reindeer. When the reindeer strayed away too far, she would merely sing one of her songs, and they would come back of their own will. She sang and sang; and when she came back to her home, she would find the fire burning, the food cooked, and everything ready. Thus she lived on without work, care, or trouble.

One day she saw that half the sky was darkened. This darkness approached nearer and nearer. It was the evil spirit. One of his lips touched the sky, the other dragged along the ground. Between was an open mouth, ready to swallow up whatever came in its way. "Ah!" said the girl, "my death is coming. What shall I do?" She took her iron-tipped staff and fled.

The evil spirit gave chase, and was gaining on her. She drew from her pocket a small comb of ivory and threw it back over her shoulder. The comb turned into a dense forest. The girl ran onward. When the evil spirit reached the forest he swallowed it, chewed it, and gulped it down. He digested it and then defecated. The dense forest turned again into a small ivory comb. After that he continued his pursuit and was gaining on her, as before. She loosened from her waist a red handkerchief, which became a fire extending from heaven to earth. The evil spirit reached the fire. He went to a river and drank it completely dry. Then he came back to the fire, and poured the water upon it. The fire was extinguished. Only a red handkerchief lay on the ground, quite small, and dripping wet.

After that he gave chase again, and gained steadily on the girl. She struck the ground with her iron-tipped staff, and all at once she turned into an arctic fox. In this form she sped on, swifter than ever. The big mouth, however, followed after, wide open, and ready to swallow her. She struck the ground with her iron-tipped staff, turned into a wolverene and fled swifter than ever, but the evil mouth followed after. She struck the ground with her iron-tipped staff and turned into a wolf and sped away swifter than ever. She struck the ground with her iron-pointed staff and turned into a bear, with a copper bell in each ear. She ran off swifter than ever, but the big mouth followed and gained on her steadily. Finally, it came very near, and was going to swallow her.

Then she saw a Lamut tent covered with white skins. She summoned all her strength, and rushed on toward that tent. She stumbled at the entrance and fell down, exhausted and senseless. After a while, she came to herself and looked about. On each side of her stood a young man, their caps adorned with large silver plates. She looked backward, and saw the evil spirit who had turned into a handsome youth, fairer than the sun. He was combing and parting his hair, making it smooth and fine. The girl rose to her feet.

The three young men came to her and asked her to enter the tent. The one who had appeared in the form of the evil spirit said, "we are three brothers, and I am the eldest one. I wanted to bring you to my tent. Now you must tell us which of us you will choose for your husband." She chose the eldest, and married him, and they lived together. The end.

Told by John Korkin, a Tundra Yukaghir man, on the western tundra of the Kolyma, spring of 1895.

2. *(A Tale about the Wood-Master.)*[2]

There lived a man who was very poor. He used to walk along a small river near his house, constructing deadfalls for hares. Sometimes he would catch one hare, another time he would catch two. With these he fed his family. One time he said to himself, "what does the Wood-Master look like? I should like to see him." The whole day long he walked about, and thought of the Wood-Master. The next morning he set off to examine his deadfalls and all at once there came a heavy snowstorm. He lost his way and struggled on not knowing where he went. At last he felt very tired, so he found a cavity under a steep bank of the river. Then he made a fire and crouched before it, waiting for better weather. All at once, not far off, he saw a huge iron sledge. An iron reindeer-buck just as big was attached to the sledge, and a black-faced man as tall as a larch tree was walking along with enormous strides. He asked himself, "what are these? I wanted to see the Wood-Master. Goodness! Is this not the Wood-Master himself, with his appurtenances?" He was so frightened that he cried aloud, "God help me!" In a moment the iron sledge broke into a number of small pieces, and the iron buck was scattered to ashes. The tall man, however, did not fall at all. He looked at the man, and called angrily, "You, man! Come here!" So the man went to the Wood-Master and awaited his words. "What have you done to my property?" cried the Wood-Master. "You have broken my sledge, you have destroyed my driving-reindeer, and you have even frightened me. I was frightened no less than you. And now you want me to walk on foot! I will not. You must repair my sledge, and restore to life my driving reindeer-buck. This is the task that you must perform." "How can I perform a task like that?" said the man. "Ah!" said the Wood-Master, "why have you been thinking about me so steadily? You were calling me in your mind, so I came. Now you must make good your evil action." "Ah, sorrows!" said the Lamut, "I will try my best, but then you must let me walk alone. I cannot achieve anything in the presence of another being, be it man, forest-owner, or evil spirit." "All right," said the Wood-Master, "you may walk alone."

Then the black giant set off. The Lamut walked around some small bushes, saying "Sledge, O sledge! Be whole again! Buck, O buck! Be whole again!" And, indeed, the sledge and the buck were whole, as before. Then he touched the reindeer-buck with his right hand. "Buck, O buck! Come to life!" But the buck remained without life and motion. He touched the buck with his left hand, and said likewise, "Buck, O buck, come to life again!" And, indeed, the reindeer-buck, gave a start, and came to life. "Ah, ah!" said the Lamut, "where are you, black giant, Forest-Owner?" At once the black giant appeared. "Oh, it is all right! What do you want me to pay you for this? I can give you immense wealth." "I do not wish any wealth at all. I want plenty of food for all of my life." "All right, go home! You shall have as much food as you want. Have no care. Go home and sleep! Tomorrow morning go into the forest, and set there five large self-acting bows. They shall give you ample food."

The Lamut went home. His wife said to him, "O husband! I thought you would never come. It is several days since I saw you last." "I was caught in a heavy snowstorm, so I sat crouching under the steep bank before a small fire." "What snowstorm?" asked the old woman in great wonder. "We have not had the slightest trace of any storm."

The next morning the Lamut went into the woods and set five self-acting bows; and that very night five big elks were killed. He took them home. After that, he would catch five elks every time. He collected a great mass of meat and a number of skins, and so became very rich. He lived in plenty until his death.

Told by John Korkin, a Tundra Yukaghir, on the western tundra of the Kolyma country, spring of 1895.

3. (Tale about the Sea-Spirit.)[3]

There was a small river that flowed into the sea. Some Tungus lived at the mouth of the river, and caught fish. One time they came to the sea and saw a sea-spirit as big as a whale coming up from under the water. The sea-spirit said, "O people! You are here. I want to devour you." They prayed to him to let them live. "All right," said the spirit, "I will devour only one man now, and the others may go home, but every day you must give me one man. You must bring him to the sea, and leave him near the water. He shall be food for me. Otherwise, if you do not do as I bid, I shall carry off your nets and drive away all the fish. I shall turn over your canoes, and so I shall surely devour you, nevertheless.

The Tungus went home, leaving one of their number behind. They went to their chief, and said to him, "what is to be done? We have to give away one man after another. We cannot live without the sea." So they gave to the spirit one victim after another. At last came the turn of the only daughter of the chief. They took her to the sea and put her down on the sand. Then they went back. The young girl sat there awaiting her death. Then she saw a young man coming. He was a wanderer, who knew neither father nor mother, and was walking around aimlessly. "What are you doing here?" said the young man. "I am awaiting my death. The sea-spirit is coming to devour me." "The sea-spirit! What is he like? I want to stay here and see him." "Young man," said the chief's daughter, "go home. What need of two human lives being destroyed?" "I have no fear," said the young man. "I have neither father nor mother. There is not a single soul in the world that would lament my death. I shall sit here and wait for the sea-spirit." He took his place close to the chief's daughter, and said to her, "rouse me a little, and make me sleep! But if anybody comes, make me get up!"

So he slept, and did not wake until the flood tide set in, and with the flood came the sea-spirit. He saw the young man, and said with joy, "Ah, good people! This time they brought two people instead of one." The chief's daughter wanted to rouse the young man; but he slept on, and took no heed of all her nudging and shaking. So she cried over him and a hot tear trickled down and fell upon his face. The young man awoke instantly and sprang up. "Ah, ah," said he, "you are already here!" He attacked the sea-monster, and they fought until late in the evening. At last the young man grasped the upper jaw of the monster, and tore it off along with the skull. "Oh, I am tired!" said the young man. He sat down again and put his head upon the girl's lap. "Rouse me again," said he, and she did so. He went to sleep as before. One of the herdsmen of the chief came to the shore. He said to the girl, "Why, you are still alive?" "I am," said the girl. "And how is it with the sea-spirit?" "This man has killed him." "You lie!" said the herdsman. "Who will believe that a loitering fellow like this man with no kith or kin, could kill the monster? It is I who killed the monster."

He drew a knife and stabbed the man. He threw his body into the sea, and said to the girl, "thus have I done; and if you contradict me with as much as a word, I shall do the same to you." She was frightened, and promised to obey him and to say that he had killed the monster. So he took her by the hand and led her back to her father. "Here," said he, "I have killed the sea-monster, and saved your only daughter from death. Your daughter is mine at present." The father was full of joy. "All right," said he, "take her and marry her." They arranged a great bridal feast for the next morning.

In the meantime, the chief's daughter called together all the girls of the village, and they prepared a large drag-net, as large as the sea itself. They cast it into the sea and dragged it along the shore, and then right across the sea. They toiled and toiled the whole night long, and in the morning at dawn they caught the body of her rescuer. "Here it is," said the chief's daughter. "This man saved me from the monster, and the herdsman stabbed him in his sleep. Now I shall stab myself, so that both of us may have one common funeral." "Do not do so," said one of her companions. "I know a rock not far from here. From under that rock comes a stream of water, scalding hot, but good for healing all kinds of wounds." She went to the rock with a stone bottle and fetched some of the water. They washed the wound with it, and, lo! the youth came to life again. The girl took him by the hand and led him to her father. "This is the man who saved me. The other one is a traitor and an impostor." So they killed the herdsman, the young man married the girl, and they lived there. The end.

Told by Innocent Karyakin, a Tundra Yukaghir on the western tundra of the Kolyma country, winter of 1895.

4. (The Sly Young Man.)[4]

There were two brothers, one married, the other unmarried. The married one lived in one place; the unmarried one, in another. They did not want to live together. One time the unmarried brother wanted to visit the married one. When he approached his house, he listened, and thought, "why, my brother and his wife are talking and laughing quite merrily." When he came nearer, however, he noticed that the man's voice was not that of his brother. So he crept along the wall very cautiously, and then looked through a rent in the skin covering. A strange man was having quite a merry time with his sister-in-law. They were hugging and kissing, and talking and playing with each other. He thought, "my brother is not here. Probably he is off hunting wild reindeer." The others meanwhile took off their breeches and made love right before him, though unaware of his presence. At the most critical moment the young man entered the house. The woman, however, shook herself free, swifter than a she-ermine, and in a moment the man too was hidden beneath the blanket. The young man said nothing. He simply sat down and waited for the evening. The other man, the one hidden under the blanket, having nothing else to do, also waited. Late in the evening, the married brother came home.

The unmarried brother said nothing to him about the strange man hidden in the house, the woman also said nothing; but both were silent and very anxious. The married brother said, "Listen, wife! Our brother has come to visit us. Cook plenty of the best meat and reindeer-fat, and we will have a hearty meal." The visiting brother said nothing, and waited, as before. The woman cooked some meat, and taking it out of the kettle, carved it with great care and spread the meal. The married brother said, "come on. Let us eat." The other answered, "how can we eat, since a strange man is hidden in our house?" The married brother said, "then I shall look for him in every corner, and certainly I shall find him." He did so, searching all through the house, but found nothing. Then he said again, "so it was a joke of yours. Come on! Let us have a meal!" The unmarried brother said, as before, "how can we have a meal? A strange man is hidden in the house." The same happened three successive times. At last the unmarried brother said, "Leave me alone! How can we have a meal? A strange man is hidden in your bed, and covered with your own blankets." The married brother pulled off the blanket. The strange man was lying there, face downward. His head was under the pillow. The married brother felt very angry. He drew his knife and with a single blow, cut off the head of the adulterer. Then he came to himself and said with great sorrow, "Oh, brother! And you, woman! You ought to have warned me in time. Now, what is to be done? I have killed a man. What will happen to us?" He sat down and cried most wretchedly. The other brother said, "what of it? There is no need of crying. He has been killed, and we cannot change it. It is better that I carry off the body and dispose of it."

He took the body and carried it off. After some time he found the tracks of the killed man and followed them up. He came to a beaten road, and then to a large village. It had numerous houses, some of them Tungus, and some Yakut. They had herds of reindeer and also of horses. In the middle of the village stood a large house just like a hill. It was the house of the chief of the village. The unmarried brother arrived there in the night time and soon found the house of the killed man. He entered at once, carrying the corpse on his back. The parents of the killed one, an old man and an old woman, were sleeping on the right hand side of the house. The bed of their son was on the left hand side. He went to the bed, put down the body, and covered it with a skin blanket. He tucked in the folds with great care, and then placed the head in its proper place, so that he looked just like a man sleeping. The old man, and the old woman heard a rustling sound and thought, "Ah, it is our son! He has come home." Then the father said, "Ah, it is you! Why are you so late?"

In another corner slept the elder brother of the killed man and his wife. He also said, "why are you so late? You ought to be asleep long ago." The man who had carried in the corpse crept softly out of the house and went home. He came to his married brother, who said, "Ah, it is you! You are alive. And what have you done with the body?" "I carried it to the house of his parents and put it down on his own bed. He ought to have slept on it long ago."

After that they had a meal. Then the unmarried brother said again, "I will go back and see what happened to the dead body." "Do not go! This time they will surely kill you." "They will not kill me. I shall go and see." He would not listen to his married brother, and went back to the house of the dead man. He approached, and heard loud wailing. The relatives of the killed man were lamenting over the body. He entered and saluted the old man. Then modestly he sat down at the women's place. The old man said, "I never saw such a face in our village. Certainly, you are a stranger, a visitor to our country." "I am," said the young man. "And why are you lamenting in this way?" "We have good reason for it," said the old man. "Two sons we had, and now we have lost one of them. He used to walk in the night time, heaven knows where. Then he grew angry with us and in that angry mood he cut off his own head. After that he lay down, covered himself with a blanket, and then he died. So you see we have good reasons for lamenting."

They had a meal and then some tea. After that the old man said, "we have no shamans in our village, although it is large. Perhaps you know of some shaman in your own country?" "Yes," said the young man, "I know of one." He lied once more. He did not know of any shaman. "Ah!" said the old man, brightening up, "if that is so, go and bring him here." He asked them for two horses, one for himself, and another for the shaman whom he was to bring. "I will ride one horse, and the other I will lead behind with a halter for the shaman." He rode off without aim and purpose, for he knew of no shaman. After a long while he came to a lonesome log cabin. Some wolflings were playing before the entrance. He entered. An old wolf-woman was sitting on a bench. Her hair was long, it hung down and spread over the floor. A young girl was sitting at a table. She was quite fair, fairer than the sun. This was the Wolf-girl. The wolflings outside were her brothers. The old woman looked up and said, "I never saw such a face in our own place. No human beings ever came here. Who are you, a human creature, or something else?" "I am human." "And what are you looking for, roaming about?" "I am in great need. I am looking for a shaman, having been sent by a suffering person." She repeated her question, and he answered the same as before. The old woman held her breath for some time. Then she said, "I am too old now. I do not know whether I still possess any power, but in former times I used to help people." He took hold of her, put her upon his horse, and rode back to the old man's home.

He took her into the house, and said, "this is the shaman I have brought for you." They treated her to the best dainties, and all the while she was drying over the fire her small, strange shaman's drum. After that she started her shamanistic performance. According to custom, she made the man who had taken her there hold the long tassel fastened to the back of her garments. "Take care!" said the old woman, "do not let go of this tassel!" He grasped the tassel, and the old woman wound herself around like a piece of birchbark over the fire. The house was full of people, house-mates, guests, onlookers. After a while the young man said, "I feel very hot. Let somebody hold this tassel for a little while, and I will go out and cool myself."

He went out of the house. The moon was shining brightly. A number of horses were digging the snow for some tussock-grass. He caught them all. Then he cut down some young willow and prepared a number of willow brooms, one for each of the horses. He tied the brooms to the tails of the horses. Then he set them afire, and set the horses free. Seeing the glare and scenting the smell of fire, they ran away in every direction. He went back and took hold of the tassel again, as though nothing had happened. Then some other person went out, and hurried back, shouting, "O men! The country all around is aflame!" And, indeed, the horses were galloping about, waving high their tails of fire. "Who lighted this fire?"

said the people. "Perhaps the spirits." Everyone left the house. They stood outside, staring upon that living fire fleeting by. "Ah, ah!" said some of them. "It is our end. This fire will burn us down." Not one of them thought any more of the old woman. The young man, however, quietly slipped back into the house.

The old woman was drumming more violently than ever. She was so full of inspiration, that she had noticed nothing at all. He looked about. No one was there. The old woman drummed on. Then he lifted from the ground a big kettle full to the brim of ice-cold water and all at once he overturned it over the old woman's head. After that he put the kettle over her head and shoulders. The old woman shuddered, and fell down dead, as is the way of all shamans when frightened unexpectedly. The young man left the house, and mingled among the people outside, looking most innocent.

After some time, however, he said, "why are we standing here looking at this blaze, and meantime we have left the shaman alone in the house? That is wrong." They hurried back, and the wolf shaman was lying on the ground, wet and stone dead, half hidden in the kettle.

The old man was in great fear, and wailed aloud, "Alas, alas! I lost a son, and that was bad enough; but it is much worse that this Wolf-woman has died in our house. Her children will surely come and wreak vengeance upon our heads. We are already as good as dead. O God!" he continued, "we are in a bad plight. Somebody must go and carry the Wolf-woman to her own house."

The people were full of fear and nobody wanted to go. Then the old man tried to induce the young visitor to convey the body of the Wolf-woman to her family. The young man said, "how can I do this? They will tear me into bits." The old man had a young daughter who was very pretty. He said, "please toss this old woman away! If you come back alive, you may marry this young girl as your reward." "All right," said the young man, "but still I am not sure. Perhaps, even if I come back alive, you will break your word and give me nothing." "No, never!" said the old man, "I will deal honestly with you." "So be it," said the young man. "Now please kill for me two ptarmigan, and give me their bladders filled with fresh and warm blood." He took the bladders and placed them under his armpits. Then he drove some iron nails into his heels, into the very flesh. He took the old woman and put her upon the saddle. Then he bound her fast, though not very strongly. She looked, however, quite like a living person riding a horse. They set off and reached the house of the wolves. "Oh," the wolflings raised a yell, "Mamma is coming, mamma is coming!" "Easy," said the young man. "My horse shies easily. Take care lest you cause some great misfortune." And he secretly spurred his horse with the nails of his feet. The horse reared and threw him down. The other horse did the same. The body of the wolf-mother fell down like a bundle of rags. The bladder burst, and all the blood was spilled. They lay there side by side, swimming in blood. The wolf-children said, "O brother! Our mother is dead; but that is as nothing. We have killed that stranger by our imprudence. He is near unto death, and no doubt his brothers and sisters, and all his kith and kin, will come here to have revenge."

They went near and looked at him. The blood was streaming down his arms and legs. "Oh, oh!" said the wolf-children, "how can he live?" In despair they took him by the hands and feet and shook him and said to him, "Please, man, do not die here! We will give you our pretty sister."They worried him, howled over him, and entreated him, and by and by he acted as though feeling a little better. He sighed low, "Oh, oh!" In the end he fully revived and came to. "Ah!" said the wolflings to their sister, "see what good luck we have. A man was dying, and we said, 'we will give you our sister,' and he revived."

So he took the girl and went home. "Be sure," said the wolf children on taking farewell, "when you return to your own place, not to tell your kinsmen that we had nearly killed you!" "I will not tell," assured the man, and galloped off with his bride. They came to the old man. "I have come back and am alive!" shouted the young man. "Where is the girl?" "Here she is," said the old man. "Thank god, you have come back safe!" He took the other girl, and went back to his brother with two women and three horses. The brother said, "How long it is since you were here! I thought you were dead but I see you have brought some girls." "I have," said the young man. He entered the house, and without much ado, cut off the head of his sister-in-law. "There you are!" said he. "You shall have no more paramours." He gave his brother the old man's daughter and took for himself the old woman's daughter. After that they lived on.

Told by Innocent Karyakin, a Tundra Yukaghir man, on the western tundra of the Kolyma country, winter of 1895.

5. (Creation Story.)

When the Creator created the earth, the bear was made the master of all the beasts. The wolf, the fox, and the wolverene paid homage to him. But the wild reindeer refused to obey him, and ran about free, as before. One day the Forest-Owner was hunting five reindeer-does; and one doe, in running, brought forth a fawn. The Forest-Owner caught it and wanted to devour it. The Fawn said, "please give me a respite. My flesh is too lean. Let me grow up to be a one-year-old." "All right," said the Forest-Owner, and he let him go.

After a year the Forest-Owner found the fawn, and wanted to devour it; but the fawn said once more, "Do not eat me now! Let me rather grow a little and be a two-year-old." "All right," said the Forest-Owner, and he let him go. Another year passed, and the reindeer fawn had new antlers, as hard as iron and as sharp as spears. Then the Forest-Owner found the fawn and wanted to devour it. He said, "this time I am going to eat you up." "Do!" said the fawn. The Forest-Owner drew his knife and wanted to stab the fawn. "No," said the fawn, "such a death is too cruel and too hard. Please grasp my antlers and wrench off my head." The Forest-Owner assented, and grasped the fawn's antlers. Then the fawn gored him and pierced his belly through, so that the intestines fell out and the Forest-Owner died. The fawn sought his mother. "Oh, you are still alive! I thought you were dead." "No," said the fawn, "I killed the Forest-Owner, and I am the chief of the reindeer." Then the bear sent a fox to the fawn. The fox said, "all the beasts pay homage to the bear, and he wants you to do the same." "No," said the fawn, "I killed the Forest-Owner, I also am a chief."

After that they prepared for war. The bear called together all those with claws and teeth, the fox, the wolverene, the wolf, the ermine. The reindeer-fawn called together all those with hoofs and antlers, the reindeer, the elk, the mountain-sheep. Then they fought. The bear and the reindeer-fawn had a single fight. The fawn pierced the bear through with its antlers of iron. Then it stood still and felt elated. But its mother said, "there is no reason to feel elated. Your death is at hand." Just as she said this, a wolf sprang up from behind, caught the fawn by the throat and lolled it.

Because the reindeer-fawn gored the Forest-Owner to death, no reindeer dies a natural death. It lives on until a wolf, creeping up from behind opens its throat and kills it.

Told by Innocent Karyakin, a Tundra Yukaghir man, on the western tundra of the Kolyma country, winter of 1895.

6. (The Shaman who turned into a Fox.)

There lived an old man who had a pretty young daughter. He was a great shaman, and he wanted to find a husband for her, the best of all human kind. So he turned into an arctic fox and ran along. Whomsoever he met, by him he would allow himself to be caught. And as soon as the man caught him, his hand would stick to the fox's back. Then the fox would rush onward, dragging the man along. The fox would come to a river and turn into a fish. Then it would dive into the water, dragging the man along. And so the man would be drowned.

Another time he turned into a red fox and ran along. Whomsoever he met, by him he would permit himself to be caught. Then the hand of the man would stick to the fox's back. The fox would rush onward, dragging the man along, and soon would drown him in the river.

A third time he turned into an ermine, and the same happened as before.

Finally, he turned into a black fox and ran along. He met a young man, a wanderer, who knew neither father nor mother, and who walked about without aim and in great poverty. The fox allowed himself to be taken. Then the hand of the wanderer stuck to his back, and the fox rushed on, dragging the man along. The fox ran to the river, turned into a fish, and dived into the water, dragging the man along. The fish crossed the river, came to the opposite shore, and turned again into a fox. And, lo! the young man was still alive. The fox rushed on, and came to some rocks. The rocks were all covered with sharp-pointed spikes. The number of the rocks was ten. The fox ran through between all of them, and, the man along with him. The man was winding along like a thin hair, and he was still alive. The fox ran into a forest, which was as dense and thick as the autumn grass. The bark of one tree touched the bark of another. They crossed this dense forest, but the young man was still alive. The fox came to the sea, and plunged into the sea. He went across the sea to the opposite shore, but the man was still alive. Then the fox said, "Oh, you are an excellent man! I want to have you for a husband for my daughter. I will let go of your hand. So please let go of my back." The man said, "I do not want to have your daughter. I want rather to have your skin." He lifted the black fox high into the air, and then struck it upon the ground with much force. The fox was dead. That is all.

Told by Innocent Karyakin, a Tundra Yukaghir man, on the western tundra of Kolyma, winter of 1895.

7. *(Tale about Three Storks.)*

There lived a man who did not know where he was born. We think, however, that we were born of this man. He was rich in everything. One time a She-Monster came to him and wanted to be his wife. The She-Monster said, "you must take me for your wife. Otherwise, I shall devour you." So he married her, and they lived together. After some time he felt sorrowful and thought to himself, "is it fair, that I being a man, so strong and rich, must have for a wife this unclean monster?"

He came to a water-hole, and sat down there. For three days and three nights he cried from vexation near the water-hole. One time, when he was crying there, a girl appeared out of the water. He said, "I am lonely. Sit down by my side and cry with me?" "How can I sit by your side? Your Monster Wife will surely kill me." The man spoke fair words to the girl. Three times she appeared out of the water-hole and talked to him. The She-Monster said, "what is the matter with you? For three nights in succession you have stayed near that water-hole. Did you not find another woman there to spend your nights with?" The man answered, "where should I find a woman better than yourself? And why should I look for another woman?" They lay down and slept together.

Early in the morning the woman arose from the bed. She threw her thimble upon the man; and his sleep grew sound and strong, almost like death. He slept throughout the day, and on until midnight. The Monster-Woman took his bow and arrows and went to the water-hole. She lay there in ambush, holding the bow strung and ready to shoot. At last, the water-woman appeared out of the water-hole. The Monster-Woman shot at her, and hit her straight in the heart. She fell down, and sank to the bottom.

The Monster-Woman came home and picked up her thimble from the man's bed. The man awoke instantly. He looked around, and said, "Ah! How long have I slept?" So he put on his clothes and ran to the water-hole. It was full of blood. He saw the blood, and cried bitterly. "Ah!" said he, "it is my wife who has spilled this blood." He plunged into the water-hole head foremost.

When he reached the bottom, it was like another earth. He looked about, and saw that every bush had, instead of leaves, small copper bells, and the tussocks were covered with sableskin instead of moss.[5] "What a fine place!" thought the man, and he walked onward along the beaten track. After a while, he came to a river. On the other shore stood a tent of Lamut type, made of silver. He came nearer and heard voices within. So he entered.

A woman lay on the bed of skins, moaning with pain. Two strong men were sitting by her, right and left. The men jumped up and laid hands upon the visitor. They shouted, "This man has killed our sister!" And they wanted to kill him on the spot; but the woman said, "Do not kill him! He did me no harm. His wife killed me." He looked at her more closely. An arrow was sticking out from her heart, and the woman was ashen from pain. She moaned pitifully, and said, "Bring him nearer!" They brought him close to the woman, and he took his place by her bed. She cried, and he cried with her. He wanted to pull out the arrow; but the woman said, "Leave it alone! I shall die at your first touch.

But if you want to restore me to life, go off across two stretches of land. In the third country you will see a silver hill and three she-storks are playing on it. You must creep close to them, and catch one of them. Then you must bring her to me."

He set off, and after passing through these two countries he saw the silver hill. Three she-storks were playing on the hill, and amusing themselves with their stork-play. He tried to creep nearer, but after some time the storks noticed him. He fell to the ground full of despair, and in his despair he turned into a little shrew. Then he heard the storks talking to one another, plainly, in the Lamut language. The youngest one raised herself on her long legs, stretched her neck, and asked, "O sisters! Where is that man? And what is coming now, so small and mouse-like?" The other said, "why do you stretch your neck in such a manner? This is no man at all. Otherwise we should have noticed him sooner than you." They flew up and circled around the hill.

In the meantime, the man had reached the top of the hill. The storks descended again; but the youngest said, "Ah! My heart misgives me. This man is hidden somewhere." But the two others retorted, "Ah, nonsense! We should have noticed him sooner than you." The two eldest ones descended to the hill; the third was still circling around in the air. All at once the shrew turned into a man, who caught one of the storks by her long leg. "Ah, ah, ah!" blubbered the stork, "and how does our other sister at home fare? Is she still living, or is she dead?" He told them everything. They were greatly moved and said, "go home, and we will follow you." He went home, and the three storks followed him on high, with much talking and many songs. He reached the house and entered it; but the storks were circling on high, singing their incantations. They wanted to pull out the arrow. The oldest said to the youngest, "Do try and pull out the arrow!" "You are older than I. You have more skill than I." "No, we are unable to pull it out. Do try to get it out!" Then the youngest stork flew upward, and for a moment stood still directly over the vent hole of the silver tent. Then she dropped down like a stone; and when half way down, she soared up again. They looked up, and the arrow was in her beak.

The patient sat up directly and wiped away the tears of pain. Then she said, "indeed, our youngest sister is a shaman." She entered the house, and also praised the man. "Your heart is true. Will you take me for your wife?" He took her for his wife, and on the bridal night they slept in the silver tent; and the three female storks were circling above all night long, keeping watch over them and singing incantations. In the morning, the storks said to their two brothers, "you must send our brother-in-law, together with his wife, back to his home." "All right," said the brothers. "Let them stay here for one day more, and then we will get them ready for the trip; but you must fly first, and see that everything in their home is in order."

The storks flew off, and came to his house; and that very evening they came back. The man said to them, "how shall we go home? I have great fear for my young bride," the storks answered. "Have no fear. We caught your old wife, and threw her into the sea. She turned into a big sea-worm." The next morning they started on their journey; and the youngest stork warned them, "Be sure not to sleep on the way!" They moved on, he in front, and his young bride close behind him, both on reindeer-back. Half way along he was overpowered with sleep. Do what he would, he could not keep awake, and at last he fell from the saddle like one dead. The wife tried to wake him and said, "did not our sisters warn us against sleeping in the way?" But he did not hear her words.

In the meantime, while she was busy over him, nudging him, and pulling him up, a big Eagle-Man with two heads came, and shouted, "I have been making suit for her since her earliest years." The Eagle-Man caught her by her tresses and threw her upon his back. Then he flew off, and carried her along. After a while the man awoke, and his wife was nowhere to be seen. He cried from grief, and then looked around. No trace was left upon the snow, he saw only their own tracks made when they were coming to that place.

The three storks arrived. The youngest one said, "did we not tell you not to go to sleep? Now what is to be done? The giant Eagle-Man is the mightiest of all creatures. They flew away in pursuit of the Eagle-Man. The young man followed behind on foot. After a while they overtook the Eagle. He was flying on, carrying the woman. Then the two elder storks told the youngest one, "why, sister, we can do nothing. You alone must try your skill and good luck. All we can do is to aid your efforts." "I will try," said the youngest stork. She flew straight upwards, and vanished from sight. Then she fell straight down upon the Eagle, and snatched the young woman from his talons; and he still flew onward, noticing nothing at all. The youngest stork put the young woman upon her back and carried her back to her husband. They prepared for the journey again. The youngest stork said, "now, you must go home. Nothing evil will befall you. You shall live there in wealth and good health. Children shall be born unto you every year. Take our blessing and go away." They went on, and came to their country. There they saw that the silver Lamut tent was standing in their own place. They entered. They lived happily and quietly.

Told by Innocent Karyakin, a Tundra Yukaghir man, on the western tundra of the Kolyma country, winter of 1895.

8. (Reindeer-Born.)

There was a Tungus man who had a large reindeer herd, and no son at all. One time he came to his herd, and saw that a doe had brought forth a fawn which looked quite human. "What is this?" asked the man. "This is a small boy," said the doe. "I brought forth for you. Take him and have him for a son." The Tungus took the boy, who grew up quickly. Every day he would swallow live reindeer, one in the morning, another at noon, and still another in the evening, three meals a day, three living reindeer. So this man, who was rich in reindeer, soon had almost none at all, and was poor. Then he felt afraid, and said to himself, "he will finish the reindeer-herd, and next it will be my turn." He left his house and goods and fled away, not knowing where he was going. He walked on for a long time. Then he saw an iron house.

In the house was a very pretty girl, so pretty that all the food she swallowed was visible though her transparent body. He thought in his mind, "Oh, I wish I had a wife like that girl!" And she answered immediately, "really, you wish it?" She knew his thoughts, though he had not uttered a single word. She called him in and gave him food and drink. Then they lay down to sleep together. He stayed in that iron house three days and three nights. On the fourth morning his wife said, "it seems that you are a runaway." He said, "maybe I am." "From whom were you running? I wish you would tell me the truth." Then he said, "I took a foster child from the herd, Reindeer-born, and I was afraid he would eat me up, together with my last reindeer." "All right," said the woman, "Have no more fear! Go back to your home. Here, take this neckerchief, and if the Reindeer-born should see you and should pursue you, run to some tree and hide behind it. Reindeer-born will not be able to catch you. And if Reindeer-born should not desist, touch the tree with this neckerchief."

The man went back and came to his house. All at once he saw Reindeer-born, who rushed straight for him. The man turned about and ran for his life. He came to a tree, and hid behind it. Reindeer-born gave chase, and ran straight into the tree, striking his forehead against it with all his might. "Ah!" said Reindeer-born, "your strength is greater than mine. I cannot make you fall." In the meantime the man took the neckerchief and touched the tree with it; and instantly the kerchief turned into iron, and its outward shape was similar to that of a saw. This saw sawed at the tree and cut it down. The tree fell and struck Reindeer-born directly upon the head. It broke his head as if it had been an egg-shell, and killed him outright. The man returned to the iron house and lived there, having the young woman as a wife.

Told by Innocent Karyakin, a Tundra Yukaghir man, on the western tundra of the Kolyma country, winter of 1895.

II
TALES OF THE LAMUT

1. Chaun Story.[6]

There was a Lamut man in the country of Chaun who went to East Cape to look for some thong-seal hides. He moved and moved, and so came to the very end of the country. He had with him his wife and also a son, young and active. All around the country was wholly deserted. Not a single trace of man was to be seen anywhere. The young man said, "I will go and look for people." The father retorted, "Do not go! You will lose your way, and in any case you will find nothing." "No, I shall find them. And I shall even take a wife among them."

He went away on snowshoes, and after a considerable time came to a river wholly unknown to him. There was a large camp there. Several tents were pitched in two clusters. In one of them lived a man who had a single daughter. He entered, and stayed with this family as an adopted son-in-law. One day the father-in-law said to him, "Let us go to the river to catch fish!"

There was on the river a large open place. They set off. The son-in-law was very light of foot. He was the first to reach the open water. Without much ado he cast into the water his fish-line, and immediately felt something heavy on it. So he pulled it up, and there, caught on the hook, was a small child, human in appearance. He was much afraid, and threw the child back into the water. After that he again cast his fish-line back into the water, and in a moment drew out another human child. He threw it back into the water, but in the meantime the other people arrived. "Why are you throwing the fish back into the water?" said the old man angrily. "If you do so, you will destroy our fishing luck and the fish is our existence. Everything will be destroyed." "Oh," said the young man, "but I caught a human child! I was afraid." "I say, it was no child, it was a fish."

"You are playing jokes on us. Better go away! I was mistaken when I called you a reliable man. Be off! You are no longer my son-in-law." They cast into the water their own fish lines, and after a while they also caught a small human child. They put it upon a long wooden spit and roasted it before the fire. Then they sat down and made a meal of it. This done, they went back.

The human son-in-law felt very angry. So he also cast

his line and angled for fish. He caught one after another, and all his fish were human. In a short time, he had collected a large heap. He covered them with sticks and stones, and went home late in the evening. "Where have you been the whole day long?" asked the father-in-law quite sternly. "I have been angling." "Caught anything?" "I covered a large heap of fish with sticks and stones." The old man was very glad. "Oh, indeed, you are the very son-in-law for me!" The spring was coming. The snow was covered with a hard crust. The old man said, "Let us go on snowshoes to hunt wild reindeer-bucks!" They went out on snowshoes, and came to a forest. The old man said to his son-in-law, "you must hide behind this large tree as we will drive the reindeer towards you, that you may kill them one by one." The young man crouched behind the tree, having his bow ready. The other people drove the reindeer toward him. He saw running past him two giant men, all naked, with long hair that reached to the ground. He was so much frightened, that he did not dare to shoot at them.

The other people came. "Well," asked the old man, "have you killed them?" "Whom must I kill? Two giant men passed by, both naked, with hair hanging down to the very ground. I did not dare to shoot at them." "Ah!" said the old man angrily, "they were no men, they were wild reindeer-bucks. You spoil our hunting pursuit. This hunt is our very life. Be off! I was mistaken when I called you a reliable man. Cease being my son-in-law! Be gone from my house and family!"

They went home. The young man was angrier than ever. He ran to the forest and looked for some trace of those human reindeer-bucks. He found tracks and followed them. At last he saw those giant naked men. They were sitting on the ground leaning against the trees, and fast asleep. So he crept toward them and tied their long hair around the tree. Then he crept off and made a large fire on their windward side. They were killed by the smoke.

Late in the evening he came home. "Where have you been the whole day long?" "I found those reindeer bucks and killed both of them." Oh, they were very glad. Now they had plenty of food, but the son-in-law could not eat it. They slaughtered for him real reindeer. One day his wife said to him, "they are very angry with you because of those ever-lasting slaughters. They are going to kill you too. You had better flee to your own country." "And will you go with me?" "Yes, I will." "And what will you eat in our land?" "I shall eat fish and reindeer meat. I want no more human flesh."

Once when she had to keep watch over the reindeer herd, she crept out of the tent quite naked. She took some new clothing from the large bags outside and put it on. They fled, and came to his father. There they made her walk three times around a new fire, and thus her mind was changed. After that they left that country and moved away. They went back to their own land and lived there.

Told by Hirkon, a Lamut man from the desert of Chaun, in the village of Nishne-Kolymsk, the Kolyma country, winter of 1896.

2. A Tale of the Chukchee Invasion.

At the time of the freezing of water some Lamut men crossed the mountain ridge near the Wolverene River. They came to the upper course of the Chogodon River and lived there. They wanted to separate their reindeer herds. In doing this, they talked among themselves. One said, "we must be very careful. From the east enemies may come to kill us and to drive our herds away." Another man, young and hasty, answered, "All right, let them come! We can kill them all." An old man, the oldest of all, whose son and son-in-law were the most active and swift of foot said, "Do not say so! You must be on your guard, and show no arrogance." Still another young man said, "you are too much afraid, a whole family of cowards. Let them come! We can destroy all of them." Another old man said, "Ah! Stop talking! The evil one is watching for every rash word. He punishes arrogant people."

After that they separated their herds and went to sleep. In the morning at dawn there came from the east enemies as numerous as fleas. Even the snowy mountains grew black with the multitude of men. They were the Chukchee. They moved on in large herds like reindeer. They attacked the tents in front, and were killing the people. At that very time those in the rear gathered a few things and moved off. They rode along. The Chukchee saw them and followed afoot, so nimble and light of foot were they.

One of the pursuers shot an arrow and hit a young woman. She sank down on the neck of her reindeer. Her husband, however, the one who first said, "we can kill all of them," only glanced back, and hastily cut off the halter of her reindeer, which was attached to his own saddle. After that he galloped on more headlong than ever.

The Chukchee followed on. Another of them shot an arrow, and hit a cradle. The infant fell out.[7] His father (the one who said, "we may kill all of them") glanced back, and cut off the reindeer halter. That done, he rode on with all possible speed. They rode across the mountain-ridge, and fled to steep rocks along the narrowest paths, so that the Chukchee sledges could not follow their riding reindeer. Whenever a pack reindeer fell down exhausted, they would not stop to take off the load, but would leave it there, load and all. At last they came to the mountains of Oloi. The pursuers were not there, so they stopped, and after a while pitched their camps.

Told by Hirkon, a Lamut man from the desert of Chaun, in the village of Nishne-Kolymsk, winter of 1896.

3. (Story about Cannibals).

In ancient times the Lamut in all parts of the land ate one another. There was an old man who had an only daughter. The neighbors wanted to eat her. So the father and mother and girl fled, and wandered off for ten days and ten nights without stopping. They crossed several ridges of hills, and from the last they saw some tents standing in a pass. They descended, and pitched their own tent nearby. The people, however, were also man-eaters, even worse then those whom they had left. Although they had large reindeer herds, they wanted to eat human flesh. A rich reindeer breeder of those people paid suit to the girl. He paid a hundred Reindeer for her, and married her.

Every day the husband slaughtered fat bucks to feed his wife with their meat. They gave her of the best fat. Oh, the parents rejoiced! A poor young man who had no reindeer of his own, and who served throughout the year, summer and winter as a herdsman to the rich owner, said to them, "there is no cause to rejoice. They simply want to fatten her before they slaughter her.

When she be fat enough, they will kill her."

And, indeed, in the night time in the very act of copulation, the husband felt with his hand of the haunches and the belly of the woman, and muttered to himself, "still not enough. Why do you not eat your fill? Eat more fat and marrow." So the woman understood. The next morning the young herdsman said, "they are weary of waiting. Soon they are going to eat her. Why do you not flee? You may do so this very night, cut a way through the cover of the sleeping room."

Indeed, in the night time they ripped open the cover of the sleeping room and ran away. They took riding reindeer and rode off. They rode for a night and a day. Then they looked back, and saw three men in pursuit. So they turned in another direction and rode on. They rode again for a night and a day. Then they looked back and saw the same three pursuers who were this time nearer than before. The father grew angry, and said, "I will attend to this." He descended from the reindeer, and slipped his bow from over his shoulder. "You ride on without me. I shall wait here for the pursuers." The path was very narrow, and led through a pass, so that the three pursuers had to ride in single file. The foremost hurried on. He did not think of any danger. He only looked ahead.

When he was directly opposite the hidden man, the latter sent forth an arrow and shot him. In the same way he slew another and still another. After that he mounted his reindeer and overtook the women. They came to another country, and lived there. The girl was married again to a rich reindeer breeder, a well-meaning man, who knew nothing of man's flesh.

Told by Irashkan, a Lamut man, on the upper course of the Molonda River, in the Kolyma country, summer of 1895.

4. *(A Tale about Stingy Reindeer-Owners).*

The short days of the year had already begun, and the cold of winter had come. Then some Lamut met to live together. They pitched their tents close to one another, played cards, and had merry talks and joyful reunions. An old shaman, who had nothing to eat, had no joy. The wealthy reindeer owners gave him nothing, so stingy were they.

One time he went to sleep without any supper, and had a hungry dream, such as the Lamut used to have. In the morning he said to the best hunter in his own family, "Let us move away! I had a dream that the wolves came and scattered the reindeer herd all over the country." So they moved away and pitched camp separately. The richest of the men had several children, and up to that time they had never known what hunger was. Still he gave nothing to the poor people.

The old shaman left him. The people in the camp played cards as usual, and laughed noisily. Then they went to sleep, the herd being quite close to the camp. In the morning, however, the reindeer were gone, and only numerous tracks of wolves were seen in the deep snow. The rich man had nothing left, not even a single riding reindeer, so he had to stay in camp with all his children and grandchildren.

The others somehow moved off in pursuit of their lost animals. His men, too, tried to search for their reindeer; but all at once a violent snow-storm came which lasted several days. It covered every trace of the reindeer in front of them, and made invisible their own tracks, behind them. The great cold caused all the game to wander off. They could find nothing to feed upon, so they were starving and perishing from famine. They ate their saddles and harnesses, the covering of the tent, and even their own clothes. They crouched almost naked within their tents, protected only by the wooden frame thereof. In ten days they had never a meal, and so at last they took to gnawing their own long hands.

The old father, however, set off again. He wandered the whole day long in the open country, and found nothing. Finally, he stopped in the middle of the desert, and cried aloud in despair. The Master of the Desert heard his voice. He came all at once from underground, and asked him, "what do you want?" "My wife and children have had nothing to eat for ten days, and they are starving to death. My hunting boots are full of holes, and I am unable to walk any longer." "Do not cry!" said the Master of the Desert, "I also am the owner of reindeer. I will give you something to eat, but you must remember the ancient custom of the Lamut. When you have food, give the best morsel to your poor neighbor." "I will," said the old man. "Is not my present trial as severe as theirs?" "Now, go home!" said the Master of the Desert, "and go to sleep. Food shall come to your house." So the old man went home. His wife said to him, "Do come and look upon this sleeping boy! He is moving his mouth as if chewing. This presages good luck." The boy was the youngest child of their elder son. "Be of good cheer," said the old man, "the worst is over. We shall have something to eat."

They went to sleep and in the morning they saw that a large herd of reindeer had come to their camp. All were gray, like the wild reindeer. Still the backs of the largest bucks were worn off by saddles. These were the riding reindeer of the Master of the Desert. The people lived on these reindeer. By and by the winter passed, and the long days of the spring came back. The people broke up their tents, and in due time moved away, as is customary among the Lamut reindeer herders. They came to a camp of numerous tents, and pitched their own tents close by the others. The old woman, however, had not learned her lesson. She was stingy as before and gave evil advice to her husband. Several poor people were in that camp. The old woman said again, "we are rich, but we must not feed these good-for-nothings. We never saw them, they are strangers. Let us rather move away from here."

So they moved off, and after some days they pitched camp alone, as before. In the morning, however, all the reindeer were gone, no one knew where. Only their tracks were left on the pasture ground. They may have ascended to the sky. The Master of the Reindeer grew angry with them because of their close hands and hard hearts. Therefore he took away his property. They walked back to camp; but the people said, "formerly you gave us nothing. You too may go away with empty hands." They went away, and soon were starved to death. That is all.

Told by Ivashkan, a Lamut man, on the upper course of the Molonda River, the Kolyma country, summer of 1895.

5. Story of an Arctic Fox.

An arctic Fox constructed a fish weir on a small river to catch fish. It was winter time, and he was at work cutting the ice. A Bear came to him, and said, "O Fox! What are you doing?" "I am arranging a fish weir for catching fish." "All right. Give me a share in the spoils." "I will not. How can I? I bring forth children by the dozen at each litter. How shall I feed them?" "Nay, nay! You must give me a share of the catch." "All right. Since you are so insistent, I will give you half. Come here! I will show you what to do." He made him sit down on the floor planks, which were all wet with water. "Sit down here and keep watch over the weir. Perhaps the ice will split. You must not stir, lest you should frighten the fish away. In due time I shall come back."

The bear sat there for three days. He was frozen to the ice. At last, on the fourth day, the arctic Fox came back. "Here, you. Fox! Come to me! You talked about the fish, but where is the fish? I am near dying of cold. At least, help me to get away, pick me off, and make me free from this ice." "Ah!" said the arctic Fox, "you are too heavy. I cannot pick you off. Here!" cried the arctic Fox, "children, come here, all of you. I caught a big fat bear for you. Come here and have a meal!" The young arctic Foxes came and bit the bear to death. They had a liberal meal, and soon the bear was gone.

After that a Wolf came. "You, arctic Fox, what are you doing?" "I am constructing a fish weir to catch fish." "Give me a share." "O, no! How can I? I have too many children. I bring forth a dozen in one litter." "I say, give me a share!" "All right, I shall give you half the catch." He made him sit down on the flanks. "See here!" said Fox, "put your bushy tail down into the water, you will catch some nice fish. But you must stay quiet, and not even move a toe. Otherwise all the fish will be scared away."

After three days the arctic Fox came back to the weirs. "Oh, oh!" cried the Wolf. "There, you arctic Fox, where is your fish? I am frozen and nearly dying of cold. Please help me get away, and pick me off!" "Ah!" said the arctic Fox, "you are too heavy. Pick yourself off." Then the Wolf turned his head and gnawed at his tail. Seeing this, the arctic Fox set off, and ran away along the river bank. The Wolf, tail-less and very angry, found his tracks, and gave pursuit, but the Fox dug a hole in the snow and lay down, feigning to be lame. "Ah, you scoundrel!" growled the Wolf through his teeth, "I will catch you and tear you into three parts. You have deceived me most heartlessly." He came to the Fox, and snarled, "Here you are! You thief! Where is your fish? I will tear you to pieces." The arctic Fox shut one eye and pretended to be blind. "What fish?" asked he innocently. "I am lame and nearly blind. My other eye is also worthless. I have not left here for a number of days." "Of course," acquiesced the Wolf, "the other one had two eyes, but still these seem to be your tracks." "How can they be mine?" said arctic Fox. "Am I the only arctic Fox hereabouts? There are ever so many." "That is right," said the Wolf. He followed another track, and caught another arctic Fox. "I have you," snarled he. "It is you who made me stick to the ice of the river." And he tore him to pieces.

Told by Ulashkan, a Lamut man, on the Molonda River, in the Kolyma country, summer of 1895.

6. *(Wolves and Men.)*

There lived some people who had no dogs at all, so they caught the small puppies of a gray fox, and brought them up. These gray foxes brought forth black and spotted dogs. Another man caught a wolfling and fed it. That wolf brought forth another kind of dog. They were long-legged, and light in color. This wolf was so nimble of foot, that it could overtake and catch reindeer and elk and any other kind of game. So its master became the richest of all the people.

At last the man said, "I am quite rich. My assistants are too many." So he ceased to pay the wolf in food and shelter. The wolf went off and called all his companions. Twenty wolves came with him, and attacked the reindeer herd. Many reindeer were killed. The man caught his bow, shot at the wolves, and killed four of them. From that time began the war between man and wolf. The end.

Told by Ulashkan, a Lamut man, on the Molonda River, in the Kolyma country, summer of 1895.

7. Bear, Wolverene, and Wolf Story.

Bear, Wolverene, and Wolf, being brothers, lived side by side. The youngest brother paid suit to the daughter of the middle one. "No," said the middle one, "how is it that you ask me for my daughter? We cannot join. You are born from the snow, and I am born from the earth." [8] Wolf grew angry and made complaint to Bear. Bear bore judgment and ordered, "if that is so, you must part." He said to Wolf, "your temper is worst of all, you shall bring forth not more than two or three children." Wolf departed sorrowfully. Bear said to Wolverene, "you have a daughter, and refuse her to suitors, so you must not bring forth more than one child." He blamed Wolverene, and said, "if you had given your daughter in marriage, our people would be more numerous, so you must meet your fate in the wooden thing."

Wolverene also grew angry, and retorted, "and you must meet your fate underground." Wolverene laid a curse upon Bear; "you must sleep throughout the winter, and your fate will come to you while you are insensible to it."

So the Bear's word caused young wolves to be born by two's and three's, and wolverenes singly. The Wolverene's word caused the Bear to sleep throughout the winter, so that hunters kill him in his sleep.

Told by Ulashkan, a Lamut man, on the Molonda River, in the Kolyma country summier of 1895.

8. (A Lamut Man Turned into Stone.)

It was told in the olden times that in the Gishiga country, on the Okhotsk side, there lived some Lamut of the Lam branch who were all rich in reindeer. One of these reindeer owners had a bad temper. He used to strike his assistants for mere trifles. One time his herd went away from their usual pasture. One of the assistants set off to look for it. He came to the pasture, which was covered with the tracks of reindeer hoofs, but farther off there was not a single track. He walked and walked and grew tired. So he came home, and said, "I could not find the herd." The master gave him a severe thrashing, and then said, "how is it that you could not find it? Where can it be? I will go and look for it myself." He came to the pasture, and walked all around it, but he also could not find any tracks outside of it. He grew quite tired. There was on the border of the pasture a boulder. He climbed it and sat down to rest. His head was resting on his hands, and so he sat thinking. All at once he heard a voice, "Biya!"[9] He sprang to his feet and looked up. High on the rock there stood an old man, large and white, as high as the sky. "O man you see me?" "I see you." "You hear my voice?" "I hear your voice." "What are you doing?" "I am resting myself." "And where are your reindeer?" "I do not know." "Ah, well! But why do you strike your assistants with so little reason? Now you must look for reindeer yourself." But the man did not stir. "Why do you strike your assistants? Is not each of them a man and a Lamut like you? Look upward! There are your reindeer." He looked up, and his reindeer were mounting up to the sky, all of them, bucks and does and fawns. He looked on, but still did not stir. "So you will stand here forever." The white one vanished. Then the Lamut came to himself, and tried to climb down; but his feet stuck to the stone. He tried to disengage them, but he was unable to do so. After a while his feet and legs were sinking into the stone.

The next morning his people came to look for him. His feet had sunk into the stone up to his ankles. They tried to pull him out, but he cried for pain, "Leave me alone! I cannot stand it. It seems that I am done for. Better go away and tell the other people." So they went and told the neighbors what had happened. In a couple of days they came back. He had sunk into the stone up to the knees. They talked to him, but he did not answer. Only the look in his eyes was still life-like. They went away, and came back in the spring. He was all stone. And so he is up to the present, and stands there upon the boulder.

Told by Ulashkan, a Lamut man, on the Molonda River, in the Kolyma country, summer of 1895.

9. (A Shaman and a Boy.)

There was a great shaman who reached a very great age. When angry he could lay his spell on any one, even upon another shaman. One time he was walking about and met a little boy, who roamed about, not knowing where to go. "Who are you?" "I do not know." "Perhaps you are a shaman." "What kind of a shaman may I be? Though, indeed, I get up in my sleep and walk about sleeping." "I shall kill you." "Do, please. I shall not resist. My father and mother are gone, and I wish to follow them." "Oh, well! Then follow me."

He took him to his house, and put a plate before him. "Sit down and let us have a match!" "What kind of a match shall we have?" "A shamanistic match. You are a shaman." "No, I am not, I know nothing." "Enough. Be quiet, or I shall kill you." He spat into his palm, and put the spittle upon the plate. It grew to a small bear not greater than a louse. "Here is my champion and where is yours?" The boy scratched his head, not knowing what to do, and, lo! a small louse fell down upon the plate, a real louse. "Ah! This is yours; all right, let them fight." The bear and the louse fought throughout the day, and the louse proved the stronger. It caught the bear by the throat and wanted to strangle it. "Let go!" cried the old man. "Leave the bear alone! I shall die." "No, I shall not do so," said the boy. "It is you who wanted to have this fight." So the louse strangled the bear. As soon as the bear died the old man fell down and died also. The boy took his wives and all his goods, and became a rich man.

Told by Ulashkan, a Lamut man, on the Molonda River, in the Kolyma country, summer of 1895.

10. (The Lamut and the Russian.)

In olden times, when the Russians were not here, the Lamut lived in the mountains.[10] They had no iron, no ax, no knife. A stone tied to a stick served as ax; a rib of wild reindeer, as knife; splinters of elk thigh bone, as spears; and a thin splinter of reindeer fawn thigh as needle. They had no kettles. They spread their meat upon stones for roasting. They melted the snow into drinking water, putting it in a reindeer stomach, which they hung high above the fire.

Then came some Russian people. They questioned our men, "who are you?" "We are Lamut." "How do you kill wild reindeer?" "With bow and arrows." "We want to see them." "There they are." One young man strung the bow and shot at a splinter of wood stuck into a high tussock quite far away, and his arrow with a point of fish bone split the slender bit of wood. "Oh, how glorious!" said the Russians. "And how do you do in spring when the snow has a thin ice crust?" "We over-take them running on snowshoes." "We want to see you do it." Another young man put on his snowshoes and ran off. He sighted a wild reindeer buck, overtook it, and stabbed it with his long spear. "Oh, glorious! Indeed, you are quite active and strong, and successful in hunting, so you must be our closest friends and assistants. You must be our best companions in every way. If some member of a strange tribe should come here with evil intentions, you must kill him without fear. You must give us assistance in every struggle against all kinds of invaders." They gave them iron knives, and axes, match-locks, and kettles, and all kinds of iron ware. "Take this, and be stronger than any of your neighbors. Chastise them according to their deserts and evil intentions." After that the Russian chief instituted the tribute and noted it down in a big black book. He gave to the young Lamut pipes and tobacco, saying, "have this to smoke, and with that smoke be first to fight, speeding ahead on your snowshoes."

Told by Ulashkan, a Lamut man, on the upper course of the Molonda River, in the Kolyma country, summer of 1895.

III.
KOLYMA TALES.

1. One-Side.

There was a family of Tungus. They lived in a tent. They had three daughters. The girk, when going to pick berries, would turn into female geese. In this form they visited the sea islands. One time they flew farther than usual. On a lonely island they saw a one-sided man. When he breathed, his heart and lungs would jump out of his side. The Geese were afraid and flew home. After some time, they had nothing to eat, so they went again to the sea islands for berries. Wherever they chose a spot on which to alight, One-Side appeared and frightened them away. At last they found a place full of berries. They descended and laid aside their wings. They picked so many berries that they could hardly carry them all. They went back to the place where they had left their wings. The wings of the youngest daughter were gone. They looked for them a long time. At last, evening came and the sun went down. It grew very dark. The two elder sisters reproached the youngest one: "probably you have taken a liking to One-Side, and you have asked him to hide your wings. Now remain here alone and let him take you!" She almost cried while assuring them that their suspicions were unjust. "I have never seen him and never thought of him." They left her and flew away. She remained alone.

As soon as they were out of sight, One-Side appeared carrying her wings. "Well, now," he said, "fair maiden, will you not consent to marry me?" She refused for a long time, then she gave in, and said, "I will!" "If you are willing," said One-Side, "I will lead the way." He took her to his house. It was the usual house, made of wood, with a wooden fireplace.[11] He proved to be a good hunter, able to catch any kind of game. Still he had only one side, and with every breath his heart would jump out. They lived together for a while, and the woman brought forth a son. The young woman nursed the infant. But One-Side did not want to stay at home. He would wander about all the time, and bring back reindeer and elk. They had so much meat that the storehouses would no longer hold it. He was a great hunter. He hunted on foot on snowshoes, for he had neither reindeer, nor horses for traveling.

One time he set off to hunt as usual. Then his wife's sisters suddenly came and carried the youngest sister and her little son off to their own country. The small boy, while carried on high, shouted, "O father! O my father! We are being carried by aunties to their home, to their home." One-Side ran home as fast as he could, but he came too late. They were out of sight. Only the boy's voice was heard far away. Then he shot an arrow with a forked head in the direction whence the voice seemed to come, and the arrow cut off one of the boy's little fingers. One-Side found the arrow and the finger, and put them into his pouch.

Then he started in search of his boy. He walked and walked. A whole year passed. Then he arrived at a village. A number of children were playing "sticks." He looked from one to another, thinking of his boy. There was one poor boy who was dressed in the poorest of clothing. His body was mangy, and his head bruised and covered with scars. First, One-Side paid no attention to him, but when he finally looked at this boy, he saw that the little finger on his left hand was missing. He snatched the finger out of his pouch and placed it beside the hand, and indeed it fitted! The poor boy was his son! "Whose boy are you?" asked One-Side. "I am mamma's boy." "And where is your father?" "I have no father. I used to have one, but now I have none." "I am your father." The boy refused to believe it, and only cried bitterly. "If my father were alive, we should not be so wretched, mother and I." The elder sisters had married and made their youngest sister a drudge in the house. "Why is your head so bruised and scarred?" asked One-Side. "It is because my aunts order me to enter the house only by the back entrance, and every time I try to go in by the front entrance, they strike my head with their heavy staffs."[12] "Let us go to your house." They arrived at the house. The boy went ahead and One-Side followed him. They came to the front entrance. As soon as the boy tried to go in, his eldest aunt jumped up and struck him with her iron staff. Then the woman saw the boy's father, and felt so much ashamed, that she fell down before him.

He entered the house. They hustled about, brought food of every kind, and prepared tea. They ate so long that it grew very late and it was time to go to bed. On the following morning, after breakfast, he said to his brothers-in-law, "Let us go and try which of us can shoot the best with the bow! You are two, and I am only one." They made ready their bows and arrows and began to shoot at each other. The elder brother-in-law shot first; but One-Side jumped upward, and the arrow missed him. The second brother-in-law also shot. One-Side jumped aside and dodged the arrow. "Now I shall shoot," said One-Side, "and you try to dodge my arrows." He shot once, and hit his elder brother-in-law straight through the heart. With the second shot he killed his other brother-in-law. Then he went back to the house, killed his wife's sisters, and took home his wife and his son.

One time he set off, as usual, to look for game. When he was out of sight of his wife, he took off the skin that disguised his true form and hung it up on the top of a high larch tree. He became a young man, quite fair and handsome, just like the sunrise. He went home and sat down on his wife's bed. While he was sitting there, he was about to take off his boots.

The woman began to argue, "Go away from here! My husband will be here soon, and he will be angry with me. He will say, 'why have you let a strange man sit down on your bed?'" "I am your husband," said he. "Why do you try to drive me away?" "No," said the woman, "my husband is one-sided, and you are like other men."They argued for a long time. At last he said, "go and look at that tree yonder. I hung up my one-sided skin on it." She found the tree and the one-sided skin, and now she believed him. Then she caught him in her arms and covered him with kisses. After that they lived happier than ever. The end.

Told by Katherine Rumiantzer, a Russianized Yukaghir woman, in the village of Pokhotsk, in the Kolyma country, in the summer of 1896.

2. A Yukaghir Tale.

Once upon a time there were some Yukaghir people. They had an only daughter, who was very active and clever. One time when she was walking about a whirlwind carried her off. It took her to the mountains. A big rock, which extended from the ground up to heaven was standing there.

The whirlwind carried her there and left her close to the rock. She sat there, and after a while she saw a bluejay flying by. "O Jay, go to my father and mother and say to them, 'your daughter asks you for some glue and a glue pot, for a line, and for climbing hooks.'" "I will not go. When you were still living with your father and mother, you were nasty; whenever I wanted to pick up some meat, you drove me away. I will not help you." A snow-bunting passed by. She said to it, "go and tell my father and mother. Your daughter would dearly love to have some glue and a glue-pot, a line, and some climbing hooks." "I will go. When you were still living with your father and mother, you were very nice. I used to come and peck at the drying meat, and you would even leave for me some spare bit or a piece of dried roe; so I will help you. My wings are young. I will bring each and everyone one of the things you asked for." And really it brought everything. The girl felt glad, and sang aloud:

O jay, blue jay!
Give me your talons
To mount the rock
And to get my overcoat.
O bunting, snow-bunting!
Give me your talons [13]

To mount the rock
And to get my overcoat.
Keyom-da, Keyom-da,
Keyom-da, Keyom-da!

After some time the whirlwind brought another girl there, and then a third one. The first one said to her fellow-prisoners, "Why, sisters! There is no use to sit here and wait. Let us try to climb the rock!" She prepared three lines and three sets of climbing-hooks. Then she threw her line upward. It caught around the stone, and she climbed up. The other two followed.

When half way up, she asked of one, "well, now, sisters, perhaps we shall find only one man there, and all three of us are going to marry him. Shall we then have quarrels and fights, as usual?" "Of course we shall," said the other. So the first one, without more ado, cut off the line; and the unhappy girl fell down and was killed. Then she asked the second girl, "well, now, sister, perhaps we shall find only one man and we shall both of us marry him. Shall we then have quarrels as usual?" "Of course we shall," answered the girl. So she cut her line, and the poor girl fell back to the ground. After that she herself climbed to the top of the rock. She was full of joy, so she danced and sang:

How active she is!
How clever she is!
She climbed the rock.
Keyom-da, keyom-da,
Keyom-da, keyom-da!

The active ones climbed to the top
The slow ones all perished.
Keyom-da, keyom-da,
Keyom-da, keyom-da![14]

The top of the mountain was a high plateau. She walked across it and after a while she saw a house, well arranged and quite large. She entered. The furniture and appurtenances were of the best, but people there were none. Along the walls stood long rows of boxes and bags filled to the brim with costly furs. She opened one box and entered it. Then she closed the lid above her, and waited for events. In the evening a man came. It was One-Side. He had one leg, one arm, one side, one eye. As soon as he entered, he said aloud, "Chimney, burn! Teapot, bubble! Kettle, cook food! Take off my boots! They are too heavy." He lay down. The chimney began to burn, the teapot bubbled, the meat in the kettle was done just right. His clothes and boots were taken off and hung up to dry. Still the girl could not see anybody. The next morning One-Side went off. Then the girl left the box, and again investigated the house. Not a living person was in it. At last behind the chimney she saw a large flint stone. She lifted it; and under it there were mice and ermine, worms, flies, mosquitoes, and all kinds of larvae, as many kinds as existed in the surrounding country. Some were sewing and some were weaving, some scraping skins, and some again currying soft hides. These were the female assistants of One-Side. The girl felt jealous and angry. She filled with water the largest kettle that she could find. She hung it over the fire and when the water was scalding hot, she poured it over the vermin, and scalded them all to death. After that she crept back into the box and waited till evening. One-Side came home, and called aloud, "Chimney, burn! Kettle, bubble! Let meat be cooked! Take off my boots! I am very tired." He waited and waited, but nothing happened. The chimney did not burn, the kettle did not bubble, and nobody came to take off his boots. "What is the matter with them? Perhaps my incantations have lost their power. Maybe I am going to die. Then let me have a last look upon my peltries. Before I die, I want to see once more my wealth, my goods, peltries, and clothes." He carried all his bags and boxes into the middle of the house and opened them one by one. At last he found the girl. "Ah, it is you!" said One-Side. "Come out! You have destroyed all my people. It seems you object to having servants and female assistants: so now just stir about yourself and make yourself useful. Get the household things ready. In the morning three reindeer herds will come to you. You must catch the driving-reindeer and harness them to the sledges, and then move away to Another place." He did not indicate the place where she was to go. Early in the morning, before sunrise, she awoke, arranged all the sledges, and was ready to move. Then the three reindeer herds came to her. She caught all the pack-reindeer and attached them to the sledges. After that she she gathered all the bones, even the smallest joints, and put them into the pouch which she hung high up on a tree.

The parents waited and waited, but the boy never came. And how could he? So they prayed to God, "O

God! Give us a son or a daughter." God heard again, and gave them a son, the very last one to be given. The boy grew up and became strong of body. He also said to his parents, "O my father and my mother! I want to know whether I ever had any brothers or any sisters?" They were less willing than ever before to tell him, lest he too should go away and perish. So he walked about and played with his bow, and at last he shot an arrow into the chinmey-hole of old woman Underskin. She went out quite angry, "why do you shoot at me. I am old and defenseless. Better shoot at Raven-Man. He took away your sister and destroyed your brothers. He is a better target for your shooting." He cried aloud and went to his parents. "Oh, father and mother! You did not want to tell me, but old woman Underskin has told me the truth. Raven-Man destroyed my brothers and carried off my sister. I shall go and look for him, no matter whether you are willing or not to give me your blessing." They wanted to keep him back, and almost died with sorrow. Still he set off. After a long journey he found the house, and his sister was sitting in it. She recognized him all at once, and cried bitterly, "why did you come? He will devour you like the others." "Let him do it! I shall not object. He ate my elder brothers, let him finish the whole breed!" She gave him food and drink, and they waited. Raven-Man flew home, and croaked, "Food, food, food!" He alighted on the roof of the house and turned into a strong man. He entered and said, "Oh, oh, oh! We heard nothing, we saw nobody; but the little Russian bone entered of its own will, not a strange man, either, my own brother-in-law. Go, wife, and bring us some iron nuts. We will have some fun with them." She brought the iron nuts, four dozen of them. They cracked the nuts; but while Raven was trying to open a single one, the young man was through with two or three. "Oh, oh," said Raven-Man, "you are a good one, O brother mine! You crack the nuts even quicker than I do." "Why," said the young man, "I crack them in the only way that I know." "All right!" said Raven-Man. "Now, wife, go and get the steam bath ready. We want to steam our little bones." So she went to the bath house and heated it. All the while she was crying most bitterly. Her whole face became swollen with crying. At last she came home. Raven looked up at her, and said, "there, woman, it seems you have been crying again. Take care, lest I swallow you some day!" "Ah, brother mine!" said the young man, "so you swallow human beings?" "Oh no!" answered Raven-Man, "it is only a little joke. Nevertheless let us go and have our steam bath. You must be tired from your long journey." So they went to the bath house; and one said to the other, "you enter first," and the other said, "you enter first. You are my guest." "And you are my host." The young man had his way and pushed Raven into the bath house. Then he set fire to it and burnt it up together with Raven. He scattered the ashes to the winds. Then he asked his sister, " where are the bones of our brothers?" She climbed to the tree and took them down. He entered the storehouse, and there was preserved a bottle containing the water of life and youth. He took the bones of the oldest brother and joined them all together. Then he sprinkled them with the water of life and youth. The first time he sprinkled the bones they were covered with flesh; the next time he sprinkled, the flesh was covered with skin; the third time he sprinkled, the young man sat up, and said, "Ah, ah, ah! I slept too long, but I am quite refreshed." "Ah!" said the youngest brother, "if it had not been for me, you would not have awakened at all." Then he did the same with the bones of the second brother, and restored him also to life. They gathered all the goods Raven had in his house, and went home, all four of them. They went to their father and mother. The old people were quite joyful, and from very joy they became ashes that were scattered around. The end.

Told by Nicholas Kusakoff, a Russian Creole, in the village of Pokhotsk, in the Kolyma country, summer of 1896.

3. Yukaghir Tale.[15]

There once lived an old man and his wife. They had an only son. They lived together for a long time. One day the old man came home from the woods and said to his wife, "O wife! I am going to die tomorrow morning. Here in the neighborhood is a small abandoned hut. Put my body there; and take with it a kettle and an ax, a strike-a-light, and some food." The next morning the old man was as if dead. The old woman cried over him; then she put his body, with everything required, upon a sledge, and hauled it to the funeral place. The boy went along, and helped his mother haul it. On the way they came to a brook. The old woman pulled across it with all her might, and at last broke wind. The old man giggled. The boy noticed it, and said, "There, mother, father is laughing!" The old woman grew very angry and struck the boy. "He is dead. How could he laugh?" They continued hauling the sledge, and after a while they came to another brook. Again the old woman pulled with great force and broke wind. The old man giggled again; and the boy said, "See here! Father is laughing." She struck him again. "Why, you liar! Our father is dead." They came to the abandoned hut, and put the old man inside. They shut the door and went away. After a few days the boy passed by the house, and he saw smoke ascending from the chimney-hole. He ran to his mother. "Mother, come! There is smoke over that hut." She went, and saw the smoke. Then she approached with great caution and looked in. The old man was making a fire. He was cooking some fat meat over the fire. Before he feigned death he had killed a big fat elk, and had hidden it in the hut; and he now was eating it all alone. The old woman went tome and said to the boy, "go and set some snares for ptarmigan. I want some ptarmigan." The boy set his snares and caught a ptarmigan and brought it to his mother alive. The old woman took the ptarmigan and plucked it well, leaving only the wings. Then she spoke to the ptarmigan as follows: "O ptarmigan! You have wings, and your talons are sharp and pointed. Now fly off to my old man, enter his hut through the chimney hole, and scratch his body with your sharp talons. Draw blood from his body with your talons." The ptarmigan flew to the hut, and dropped into it through the chimney hole. It attacked the old man and lacerated his body with its sharp talons. The old man was much frightened. He left the hut and ran home to his old woman. He came to the house, but the door was shut tight. He said in the Yukaghir language, "Oh, there, old woman! Open the door!"[16] "Why should I open it? You are not my old man. My old man is dead." "No," said he, "I am really your old man." "How can that be? From which world, then, did you come, from this one, or from the other one?" "So help me God! I am really your old man." She opened the door and then snatched the poker and beat him on the head. "Mind you do not eat alone without your old woman!" The old woman swore that he should never do that again. He brought home the elk carcass, and they continued to live together. That is all.

Told by Katherine Rumiantzev, a Russianized Yukaghir woman,
in the village of Pokhotek, in the Kolyma country,
summer of 1896.

4. A Bear Tale.[17]

A clan of the Tungus lived in three tents. The family in the first tent had two daughters. The elder daughter was married, and the younger lived at home. She was very pretty; and her parents made her sit in her sleeping room all the time, lest any strange eye should behold her beauty. An old woman lived with her, who gave her drink and food, and acted as a nurse. Even her parents rarely visited her. Once in a while in the night time she would go noiselessly to their sleeping room to be caressed by them.

One time when she was sitting alone in her sleeping room the lower edge of the cover was lifted up. No human hand appeared, but the flap of the cover continued to be lifted up, and at last there appeared a bear's muzzle. The girl was so badly frightened that she could not cry. The bear entered the sleeping room as far as his belly, and then caught the girl. He covered her mouth with his huge paw, and carried her off to his lair. It was in the middle of the fall; so he put her into the lair, and went in himself. He stopped up the entrance, as bears do, and they slept. They slept most of the time, but sometimes the girl would wake up and feel hungry. Then she would make known to the bear by signs that she wanted food. He would growl, stretch out one of his paws toward her, and she would suck at the thickest part of it. After she had sucked a while, fat would drip from it. She felt satisfied and went to sleep again. One time, as the days grew longer, the girl was awakened by a heavy weight that was pressing her down. She was unable to resist, and so became the wife of the bear.

At last the warm season came again. The bear left his lair and roamed about, looking for food. Every day he brought back all kinds of game, reindeer, hare, or at least ptarmigan. He never came home without something. He ate the raw meat. She could not eat it. So she prayed to the bear, "O bear! Grandfather.[18] You see I cannot eat raw meat. How shall I subsist? Please bring me some fire!" He let forth a growl and set off. For a long time he did not return. Then he brought in his mouth a fire-brand. He procured a knife and an ax (goodness knows where he got them! And, moreover, he brought her large masses of every kind of meat. She made a fire, and roasted the meat on wooden spits. On this she lived all the time.

All the snow had melted off, and patches of last year's berries appeared. She roamed about, picking berries for her own food and also for the bear. Once she heard a human voice. She hurried to the place whence it came. It was the voice of her brother-in-law. He was a great shaman, and since the fall had been looking for her on land and on water, but had found no trace of her. Now she heard his call. She hurried to the spot, pretending, however, to pick berries along the way. He came toward her, and they met, "what is the matter with you?" asked the shaman. "Who caught you and carried you away?" She answered, "A bear carried me away, and made me his wife. He keeps me close to the lair, and does not allow me to wander far away." "Ah!" said the man, "even now when you go back, he will be very angry, and he will give you a severe thrashing with his heavy paws. Then you must say to him, 'O, grandfather! Why do you beat me thus? The berries are getting scarce, and, moreover, I feel a great longing for my parents and family, and this makes me restless.' Be that as it may, you must come again to this place." Then she went back. The bear was very angry. He pawed the ground and threw it about in great lumps. Then he caught the woman and gave her a severe thrashing. The woman said, "O, grandfather! Why do you torture me so? The berries are getting scarce, and, besides, a longing for my people overpowers me. I am growing restless, and cannot stay in the same place." The bear ceased beating her. The next morning she awoke and prepared some food for herself. She ate her meal, and then set off, pretending to go berrying. As soon, however, as she was out of sight of the bear, she ran as fast as her legs would carry her to the place where she had met her brother-in-law who was already there expecting her. He said, "you must run on with all your might." He dropped to the ground, and turned into a big bear with a bell on his left ear. He rushed off to meet the other bear. On his departure, he said to her, "run as fast as you can, but in running try to listen behind you. When the earth begins to tremble and to sway right and left, then know that we have met. Listen to the bell! If it rings with a full sound, then know that I have conquered; but if the sound grows fainter, then it be that he has vanquished me. Know then that you will not live." She ran off, but tried to listen. At last the ground trembled. The bell was ringing quite loud; but gradually the sound grew fainter and fainter, and then ceased altogether. "Oh," thought the woman, "we are lost!" She ran off in more haste than ever. Then all at once the bell sounded again, stronger and stronger. Her brother-in-law had vanquished the other one and was coming back. She arrived at home, but did not enter neither the sleeping room of her parents nor her own. She entered the sleeping room of her sister who was sleeping. She fell down at her side and lost consciousness. Her brother-in-law arrived soon after her and resumed the form of a man. He awakened his wife and their parents, and they tried to restore the girl. She was very ill, however, and swooned again and again. The bear spirit was tormenting and oppressing her. After three days she came to, and in a few months she gave birth to a boy, who had bear-ears. This boy grew up and became a strong hunter. His name was Bear-Ear. That is all.

Told by Nicholas Kusakoff, a Russian creole in the village of Pokhotsk, in the Kolyma country, summer of 1896.

5. *Grass-Blade Girl.*

An old woman lived all alone. She had no children. One time she went for a walk. She saw a patch of yellow grass. One blade was growing higher than any of the others. She gathered that grass for her bedding, and kept this long blade separately. She carried the grass home, put it under her mat and slept over it. In the night time the long blade became warm from the heat of her body. In the morning the old woman mounted to the roof to open the chimney hole. Then she heard something crying in the house. It was the grass-blade which had turned into a little girl. The old woman swathed her in thin skins, fed her and nursed and caressed her. Thus Grass-Blade-Girl lived in her house and grew up. When the time came for her to be married she was a wonderful girl. When she wept her tears were costly pearls. When she smiled, her smile was all precious stones. She would swing her right sleeve, and sables and martens would drop from it. She would swing her left sleeve, and red foxes would fall out of it. She was also very pretty. The like of her was not to be met. A strong young man heard about her, and went to pay suit to her.

On his departure, he told his brothers, who had remained at home, to make arrows and to feather them well, that he might shoot with them sables and foxes for his future bride. He ordered them also to prepare bags for the skins, and boxes for the precious stones and pearls.[19]

He went to the old woman and saw the girl. She was all that people had stated her to be. Pearls and precious stones dropped from her mouth, sables and foxes fell from her sleeves. He offered his suit, and was accepted.

Then he married her and took her to his house. On the way, they passed the house of Yaghishna. Just as they were right opposite it, the bride said, "Oh, my dear! I am very thirsty. Bring me some water." He took the ice-pick and went to a lake. He cut through the ice, but there was no water. The bottom was dry. He tried another place, and still another. There was no water anywhere, and at last he went so far toward the middle of the lake, that he disappeared from the sight of the woman. In the meantime the dogs of the team scented the house of

Yaghishna. So they rushed off with the sledge, and she could not keep them back. They arrived at Yaghishna's door. The witch came out, took the young woman by the hand, and led her into the house. She made her take a place on a new reindeer skin, and went to prepare some food and hot tea for her; but when she took the first cup of tea, the witch unexpectedly pulled out the bedding from under her seat, and the young woman fell into an underground cellar a hundred fathoms deep, a hundred fathoms wide, and quite dark.

She prayed and prayed to be let out: "O grandmother! Help me out! I will give you anything you may ask of me." "All right," said the witch, "take off your clothes and give them to me, then I will help you out." The young woman took off her clothes, saving only her undershirt, and made them into a bundle. The witch dropped a long line into the cellar. The young woman tied the bundle to the line. The witch pulled up the bundle, put on the clothes, and all at once became exactly like the young bride. So she took her place upon the sledge, and hurried back to the former place. After some time the husband came. He brought some water, but the bride refused to take it. "I do not want it.

I did not ask you at all to fetch any water." They even had a quarrel. "Why," said the young man, "you were so thirsty. Have I not cut the ice maybe in twenty places to get water for you?"

After that they continued on their way. When they reached home all the people gathered to look upon the bride; but she had neither pearls nor sables. She coughed and spat, blew her nose; and only once a small glass bead fell down, which, moreover, was pierced awry. In due time, however, she bore a son. Her husband was an excellent hunter. He brought home geese and swans, reindeer and elks. The house was full of meat and of all kinds of skins. He passed most of his time in the open air, and paid no attention to the ways of his wife with their little boy. One time, however, he came home, and his wife prepared some dinner for him. While waiting for it, he took up the boy, who began to cry. "There," said the man, "the boy is crying. It is time to give him some food." The witch took the boy and turned her face toward the wall. After that she began to take off her left boot. He looked on with great wonder, and thought, "what is this? I wanted her to suckle the boy, and she takes off her boots." The woman took off the boot, and instead of the breast she gave the boy her left heel to suck. He was very angry. "Why," said her husband, "is this the way you feed our boy? Truly, you have grown up in the wild country, and you are of wild blood. You are good for nothing. I took you for a treasure, and instead you are an unclean thing. You suckle your boy in this unhallowed way. Tomorrow morning I shall take you back to your mother. I do not want you any longer." They quarrelled all night long, and did not sleep. The next morning he carried her back to her mother. They arrived there, and lo, Grass-Blade-Girl was living with the old woman again.

She had been left quite naked in the underground cellar of Yaghishna's house. When groping about in the cellar, she found it full of dead bodies of men and women. She heaped them up and mounted to the top. In this way she succeeded in making her escape. The Witch, though living far away in the house of the young man, became aware directly of the flight of her prisoner. She sent some bears and wolves in pursuit, which overtook the fugitive. They tore her to pieces, and the blood flowed all over the ground. A new thin yellowish-green grass grew up from the blood. The old woman found the grass, and gathered it; and so again she had in her house the same Grass-Blade-Girl, as before.

The young man carried his wife back to her mother, and found there also this Grass-Blade-Girl. He recognized her immediately as his former bride. They had supper, and then lay down to sleep. The old woman said to Grass-Blade-Girl, "tell us a tale." So the girl began, "there lived an old woman. She found a yellowish-green grass blade and took it home. She put it under her bedding. The next morning she went out to open the chimney-hole, and something was crying within the house. The grass-blade had turned into a little girl. The girl grew up, and a young man came and married her. He took her to his house. On the way she asked for a drink. The bridegroom went for some water. Near the trail stood the house of Yaghishna. The dogs scented it and rushed there."

As soon as she reached this place in the story, Yaghishna grew angry and interrupted her. "Enough of your prattling! We want to sleep. No need of your silly tales!" "Not so fast," said the husband. He took Yaghishna and with twelve new arrows he shot her dead in front of the house. Then he carried Grass-Blade-Girl to his house. The end.

Told by Katherine Rumiantzev, a Russianized Yukaghir woman, in the village of Pokhotsk, in the Kolyma country, summer of 1896.

6. The Alder-Block.[20]

There lived an old woman who had neither son nor daughter. One time after cooking her supper, she climbed to the roof of her house to stop up the chinmey hole. Then she heard from within a small child's voice. She was much frightened, but still she descended hastily and ran into the house. An infant boy was lying on the floor. She swathed him in swaddling clothes, and prepared food for him. She fed him on blood soup and minced meat, and he grew from year to year. She gave him the name Alder-Block. He was an excellent carpenter, and made excellent canoes of boards and of hollowed tree trunks. One time he said to his foster mother, "mother, give me permission to leave. I want to visit all the wonders of earth and sea." The woman said, "how can that be? And who will then procure food for me? You are almost full-grown. All my hope lies in you." Nevertheless, he left in the night time and went away along across the sea. He traveled and traveled, and at last he saw an island. On the island there stood a house. In it lived the witch, Yagha.[21] She had three daughters, one Five-Eyes Girl; another, Six-Eyes Girl; and the third, Eight-Eyes Girl. She herself had ten eyes. The witch Yagha saw the canoe, and said to her daughters, "Here, girls! Get ready! A small reindeer is coming from the sea. Do try and lure it hither." The eldest daughter cooked flour-cakes. She filled a birchbark vessel as big as a man with them, and put it on the shore as a decoy. She hid herself near by in order to catch the boy as soon as he should land. The boy saw the birchbark vessel full of cakes. He came close to the shore, and said aloud, "First eye, fall asleep! Second eye, fall asleep! Third eye, fall asleep! Fourth eye, fall asleep! Fifth eye, fall asleep!" The girl fell asleep. He emptied the birchbark vessel into his canoe. He threw the vessel into the water, approached the shore, and, taking off his breeches, he defecated upon her head. After that he struck her back with the paddle, and broke her back. That done, he paddled away across the sea, back to his mother. So he brought to his mother all those cakes. She was much astonished. She asked him, "O child, Alder-Block Boy! Where did you get all these cakes?" "At such and such a place."The boy told her everything. The old woman was very much scared. "Now," she said, "I will not let you go even one step from my side. The witch Yagha will devour you." That very night, as soon as the old woman had fallen asleep, Alder-Block descended toward the water, boarded his canoe, and set off again. The girls saw him, as before. They prepared a vessel with cakes, and put it out on the shore. The second sister hid nearby, ready to catch him. He paddled to the shore, and called out aloud, "First eye, fall asleep! Second eye, fall asleep! Third eye, fall asleep! And fourth and fifth and sixth eye fall asleep!" Again, the girl fell asleep.

He emptied the vessel into his canoe. Then he defecated upon the girl, and broke her back with a blow of his paddle. Then he paddled back across the sea with his booty. The girl, however, came to, and crawled to her mother. The mother sprinkled her with the water of life and youth, and the girl became as sound as before.

The boy's mother took the cakes, but she reproached him. "O, child, you go away secretly in the night time. I shall lose you and shall not know where to find you. The witch Yagha will devour you. Do stop these awful doings!" The very same night the boy went again. This time the youngest daughter tried to catch him. She also put upon the shore a vessel full of cakes, and hid nearby. He paddled shoreward, and counted aloud, "First eye, fall asleep! Second eye, fall asleep! Third eye, fall asleep! Fourth and fifth and sixth and seventh and eighth, do fall asleep!" He took the cakes and defecated upon the girl. Then he struck her with the paddle upon the back and paddled away. The girl could hardly crawl back to her mother. The next day he came again. This time it was Yaghishna herself who tried to catch him. She put the vessel upon the shore and hid nearby. He counted aloud, "First eye, fall asleep! Second eye, fall asleep! Third and fourth, fall asleep! Fifth and sixth and seventh, do fall asleep! Eighth and ninth, do fall asleep!" But he forgot the tenth eye. He took the vessel and emptied it into his canoe, but the witch did not stir. He took off his breeches and wanted to defecate upon her; then she caught him by the breeches and carried him home. "There you, dogs, you could not catch this small reindeer, but I have caught him." They had an oven dug in the ground. The Yaghishna said, "I will call my brother; meanwhile cook this reindeer for our meal. When brother and I come back, we will have a meal of him." She set off. The eldest daughter brought an iron shovel, and said to the boy, "well, Alder-Block, sit down on the shovel." He spread his legs and stretched his arms. She tried to put him down into the oven, but could not do it. " Why," said she, "Alder-Block, you hold your body too clumsily. Sit down on the shovel, then draw up your legs and keep your arms together." "How together? I do not know how. You had better show me how." "Look here, you booby!" She took a seat on the shovel and held her body quite close. So he thrust her into the oven, snatched the shovel back, and shut the oven door. In this way he killed the eldest daughter of Yaghishna. The second daughter came and asked him, "Oh, Alder-Block, what makes it smell so strong here of something singed?" "It does indeed," said Alder-Block, "your sister singed a leg of mine, and also an arm, but in the end took pity on me and allowed me to live." "I will show you what pity is. Sit down on the shovel, go your way down into the oven." He spread his legs and stretched his arms just as before. By no means could she thrust him down the oven. "Oh, there! Alder-Block, you hold yourself quite in a wrong way. Draw up your legs and keep your arms together." "How together? I do not know how." "Even so, you booby!" She sat down on the shovel and drew up her legs. He immediately thrust her down into the oven and shut the oven door. There she was roasted. The third one came too, the youngest one. "You, there, Alder-Block! Why does it smell so here of something singed?" "Yes, it does," said Alder-Block. "Your second sister singed a leg of mine, and then also an arm. Then she took pity on me and let me live." "Oh, I will teach you what pity is! Sit down on the shovel, go your way down into the oven." He spread his legs and stretched his arms. She could not thrust him in. "Oh, there, Alder-Block! You do not hold yourself right. You must draw up your legs and keep your arms together." "I do not know how. You must show me how." She sat down on the shovel, and he thrust her into the oven. After a while all three were done just right. He took them out of the oven, and drew them up to the ground. Then he prepared the meal, cut the meat, and laid it out on dishes and in troughs. All these he arranged on a large table. He put the table near the large bed of Yaghishna, where she usually took her meals and concealed all three heads under the bed near her seat. He hid himself behind the chimney and waited for Yaghishna. After a while she came back. She was driving the mortar, urging it with a pestle, and effacing the traces of the sledge with a big broom. She had not found her brother at home. So she came all alone. She entered the house, and saw the food all ready for a meal: so she felt gratified, and exclaimed, "See there! My daughters have prepared the meal, and they themselves are gone, perhaps for a little walk." She took a seat near the table and tried to eat, but the first mouthful stuck in her throat. "Oh, oh, oh!" said the witch, "what is the matter? Why does even the first mouthful stick so in my throat? Is it possible that Alder-Block is a kinsman of mine?" She took another morsel, but could not swallow it at all. She spat it out, and looked down under the bed, and there were the three heads of her daughters. She clapped her hands and wailed aloud, "Ah, you hound, Alder-Block! You have eaten all my daughters, and none has stuck in your throat." She looked around, and found the boy behind the chimney. "Ah, ah, now I have you." She caught him by the nape of the neck and hurled him across the room and back again. After a few kicks and pushes, he felt nearly dead. Then he called

aloud, "O, granny! That is enough. I want to ease myself before I die." "Go, then,
and ease yourself." He ran to her storehouse. She had there two wells, one full of water of life and youth, the other full of water of death. He drank his fill of the water of life and youth, then he changed the places of both wells. After that he came back. He caught Yaghishna and threw her across the room and back again. After a few kicks, she felt very feeble, and asked of him, "O, Alder-Block! I want to ease myself." "All right, you may go." She went to the storehouse, and wanted to drink of the water of life and youth, but instead she drank of the water of death. After that she went back, hardly being able to move. As soon as she stepped over the sill, her belly burst, and she dropped down stone dead. The boy gathered all her wealth, the costly furs, dried meat and fish, and all kinds of provisions and took it to his mother. He also took along the water of life and youth. His mother drank of the water and became quite young, like a fresh berry. He became immensely rich. The end.

Told by Katherine Rumiantzev, a Russianized Yukaghir woman, in the village of Pokhotsk, in the Kolyma country, summer of 1895.

7. Yukaghir Tale.

There lived a man with his wife. They had a daughter. The name of this daughter was kept secret. The father announced that whoever should guess her name should have her for a wife. There came traders and hunters and all kinds of able young men, but nobody could guess her name.

The couple had only a single female servant. The suitors were too many, and the housework was too hard for her. The servant had to fetch water, chop wood, and cook food. Throughout the day and night she had no rest at all. She toiled and toiled. One time she went to an ice hole in the river to draw water, feeling wearied and unhappy. She wept and a tear fell down straight into the water. At the same time she whispered to herself: "what is her name? They cannot guess it. Her name is, Kutika Mutika." All of a sudden some air bubbles danced on the water; and a Monster appeared from the ice hole, clad in hareskin.

So the Monster inquired, "what was it you whispered

when crying over the ice hole?" At first the girl refused to answer; but after a while she said, "it is so and so. I feel wearied almost to death. And what is in her name, that they cannot guess it? Her name is simply Kutika Mutika." The monster jumped out of the water and rushed off, so that the ice resounded. He came to the house of the girl. All the people laughed at him, "this ugly old man also wants to guess her name." He hopped around on one leg, and said, "her name is Spoon, her name is Ladle, her name is Big Fork, her name is Kettle-Hook." Then suddenly he said, "her name is Kutika Mutika." All the people jumped up in wonder. The old father slapped himself on the mouth with the palm of his hand. The other suitors from mere shame and anger, left immediately without waiting for dinner to be served. The old Monster remained there. The next morning they were married. The father of the girl was wealthy and generous. He had a winged horse with a natural saddle and a natural bridle. He gave this horse to his daughter as her dowry, so she mounted it. The Monster held the halter and led the way down the river directly through the ice hole. He went down, and she followed him. They descended into the river and found a trail. They followed it for a long time. At last the girl said, "O, old man! I feel hungry and thirsty. Is it still far to your houses?" "Why," said the Monster, "look there! Our houses are there." She looked, and saw a number of large bunches of grass which were standing like so many houses. From under every bunch smoke ascended. He took her to the largest of the bunches and helped her down from her horse. All kinds of monsters jumped out from under the grass. One had no trunk of the body, another was without a nose, a third even without a face. Last of all there jumped out a one-eyed old woman clad in hareskin. She hopped about on one leg, and cried, "Oh, oh! He has brought a reindeer and a doe withal." The young woman was frightened, so she cut the halter of the horse. The horse immediately flew up. It bolted through the ice-hole back to earth. It did not go back to the house of the bride's father, however, but flew on steadily. The old Monster followed it, running below. After a long time the Monster was left behind. Then he shouted with all his might, "Mind, woman! You will marry somebody else, and you will have three children by him. The first one shall be a boy, and the second a girl, and the third again a boy. Bear in mind that then I shall come to you again!"

She wandered on, and came to a wild country unknown to any one. There she married a man, who was a mighty hunter. Not a single living thing could escape his skill. They had three children, a boy and a girl, and again a boy. When the last was still an infant in the cradle, the husband one day said to his wife, "give me your horse, I want to use it to go hunting." The woman said, "Take the horse! But be careful when stopping in the woods! Tie it only to an old dry tree. Be sure not to tie it to a green tree."

He used the horse once, twice, several times. At last one day he went into the woods. About the middle of the day he stopped for dinner, and quite forgot his wife's warning about tying the horse, and tied it to a green tree.

In the meantime the woman busied herself about the house. She cooked food, then she raked up the burning coals and covered them with ashes, as is customary. The children were playing near the fireplace. All of a sudden something fumed and smouldered among the coals. She thought it was the children's fault: so she grew angry, and said to the older boy, "Now, just scrape that off with a piece of wood and throw it on the floor!" He scraped it off on to the floor; and, lo! there was the Monster, clad in hareskin, sitting near the fireplace. She was so frightened that she nearly had a fit. Then she came to herself, and said, "I will bring some food from the storehouse." She went off, and the older boy followed her. The Monster said, "Be quick! Hardly step out of the house, and you are back again!" So she took off one of her boots and squeezed it between the door and the doorpost. They had in the storehouse an old box clamped with twelve iron hoops. The woman said to the box, "you were a box clamped with twelve iron hoops. Now become a raised storehouse with twelve iron supports, and every support as thick as a man can embrace!"

So the box turned into a storehouse raised on twelve supports, each support as thick as a man could embrace. The woman and the boy were on top of the storehouse. Then she shouted, and called for her husband; but he was so far away, he could hardly hear her voice. When he heard it, he ran for the horse; but the horse had been left in the woods quite a way behind. The horse also tried to make itself free, but the green tree held it fast, notwithstanding all its efforts. The Monster went out of the house, and saw the iron storehouse. He grew very angry. First of all, he caught two of her children and swallowed them. The girl's legs just passed through his mouth like a flash. "You also shall not escape," said he, and began to vomit. After a few efforts he vomited out a large ax and attacked the iron supports. He chopped at them with supernatural force, and big iron splinters flew about. At this time a little She-Fox came and said, "O, granny! You are so tired, let me relieve you and chop a little in your stead!" He gave her the ax. She ran away and threw it into the sea. The monster vomited again and threw up a hatchet. With this he chopped at the supports with greater force than before. The Fox thought a little, then she wallowed in white clay and turned white, just like an arctic fox. She came to the Monster, and said again, "O granny! You are so tired, let me work in your stead for a while!" "And who are you?" asked the Monster. "Methinks you are the same fox." "Oh, no!" said the Fox, "don't you see! I am an arctic fox." He gave her the hatchet, and the Fox threw it into the sea. The Monster vomited again and threw out a large lance. With this he chopped at the iron supports harder than ever. Eleven supports were cut down.

Only the last was left, and the storehouse swayed to and fro upon its base. Then the winged horse with a last effort uprooted the green tree and ran home. It rushed straight to the storehouse and with its iron hoofs it broke the Monster's back. Then the husband also came home. He cut up the Monster and chopped its body into small pieces. He put what remained on a leather sledge cover and dragged it toward the sea. Then he threw all the remnants of the Monster's body into the sea. After that they left, and wandered to another country. They lived there and had more children.

Told by Nicholas Kusakoff, a Russian Creole, in the village of Pokhotsk in the Kolyma country, summer of 1895.

8. Tale about Cu'mo.

There were three sisters. They knew no men, and subsisted by hunting wild reindeer. They also wandered about gathering roots and berries and every sort of thing that the earth produces. One time the eldest sister said, "I wish we had at least one baby." As soon as she spoke these words, she glanced at a rock, and saw a severed piece which had a human face and looked like a baby. "Ah, sisters!" exclaimed the girl, "come here and see! I have found a baby in the rock." So they took the child of the stone and carried it home. They made a cradle, and put the baby in it. Then they rocked the cradle with much zeal.

After a while the baby began to cry and became like a human being.

The next day the two elder sisters went, as usual, to hunt wild reindeer, but they left the youngest sister at home. "Stay at home and nurse the infant," they said to her.

As soon as they went away, the baby began to cry louder and louder. At first the girl rocked the cradle, but the baby was not to be thus silenced. At last a sudden fright seized her without any apparent reason. She could not stand it, so she hid herself under the bed and tried to listen to what would happen next. The baby cried as before. Then it ceased, and seemed also to be listening for something. It was listening to hear whether anyone might suddenly enter. Then quite unexpectedly the baby said with a deep man's voice, "Cu'mo, Cu'mo, make yourself large!" In the same instant, it left the cradle and rose to its feet. It said again, "Cu'mo, Cu'mo, make yourself large!" And lo, its head reached the very roof. It gathered all the dried meat and fat, sausages and tongues, hanging from the rafters, and devoured all this most ravenously. Then it heard some voices. They were those of two elder sisters coming home from hunting. In the same moment it said aloud, "Cu'mo, Cu'mo, make yourself small!" So it became quite small, and was lying in the cradle and crying, just as before. The youngest sister, however, came out of her hiding-place and ran with all her might to meet the other sister. "O elder ones!" she sobbed out, "I will not stay at home alone any longer. You may stay there yourself if you want to." "What is the matter with you?" asked the eldest sister. "It is thus and so," answered the youngest one. The eldest sister was very angry. "You certainly are not telling the truth. How can a baby leave the cradle and make itself large?" The next morning, however, the youngest sister refused to stay, so the eldest sister ordered the second one to stay at home in her stead. The other two went away hunting. The girl stayed at home and rocked the cradle; but the baby cried incessantly, and at last a great fright took possession of her, quite unaccountable, and she too hid herself under the bed and listened for what would happen next. The child cried and cried. Then it became still, and also began to listen. Nobody came, however, so the baby said again with a man's deep voice, "Cu'mo, Cu'mo, make yourself large!" At that very moment it dropped to the floor and rose to its feet. Then it said again, "Cu'mo, Cu'mo, make yourself large!" and its head reached to the roof. It gathered all the dried meat and fat, sausages and tongues, hanging from the rafters, and devoured them most greedily. Then it heard human voices. They were those of the two other sisters, who were coming home and talking to each other. It said instantly, "Cu'mo, Cu'mo, make yourself small!" and all at once it was small again and in the cradle, as before. The middle sister crept out of her hiding-place and ran out to meet the sister. "Oh," said she, "it is too awful! I will not stay here any longer." "And what is the matter with you?" asked the eldest sister. "This and this," said the middle sister. "Oh, please! Enough of this! How can a little baby leave the cradle and become large?"

The next morning, however, the two younger sisters

refused to stay at home: so the eldest sister remained. The two others went off hunting reindeer. The eldest sister rocked the cradle; but the baby cried and cried, and at last there came over her also without any cause a terrible fright and she hid under the bed and listened for what might happen next. The baby cried and cried. Then it stopped and began to listen. Nobody came, however: so it said aloud with its deep bass voice, "Cu'mo, Cu'mo, make yourself large!" It dropped to the floor and rose to its feet. Then it said again. "Cu'mo, Cu'mo, make yourself large!" and its head reached the roof. It gathered all the dried meat and fat, sausages, and tongues, hanging upon the rafters, and ate them all. Then it heard distant voices. The two other sisters were coming home. So it said very quickly, "Cu'mo, Cu'mo, make yourself small!" and it was again small and lay in the cradle. The eldest sister left her hiding place and hurried to meet the other sisters. "Oh, indeed! You were quite right. It is awful! What shall we do?" They talked for a long time, trying to find a way to get rid of Cu'mo. At last they took a kettle and filled it with reindeer meat. They hung it over a large fire to cook the meat. When the meat was done, they took it out, leaving the liquid and the fat to boil in the kettle.

Then the eldest sister took the baby in her arms and said in a caressing way, "Look up there! A birdie is passing there." The baby looked up, and at that moment the girl threw it into the kettle. They had nine driving reindeer: so they left behind everything else they had, and, taking these nine reindeer, they fled. Each sister drove one reindeer, leading the other two behind her sledge as relays. They hurried off at top speed. Cu'mo went in pursuit, kettle and all.

The fire was burning, the kettle was bubbling, the iron sides were clattering as Cu'mo gave chase to the three sisters. After a while he approached them. Then the youngest sister took her ivory comb and said to it, "O comb of ivory! You were a comb, now turn into a mountain of ivory, from earth to heaven, and from east to west." She threw the comb back over her shoulder, and it turned into a big mountain, from earth to heaven, from east to west. It was just behind them: so they stopped close to it, took a rest, and ate a meal; then they attached fresh reindeer and hurried on. Cu'mo came to the ivory mountain and began to gnaw at it. Splinters of ivory flew in every direction. He gnawed it through, and went across, kettle and all, and gave chase again.

The youngest sister said, "Here, my sisters! Put your ear to the ground. Perhaps he is pursuing us again." They put an ear to the ground, and indeed the kettle was clattering quite close behind. Then the second sister took out a piece of flint. She said to the flint, "O flint! You were a piece of flint. Now turn into a mountain of flint, from earth to heaven, from east to west." Then she threw the flint back over her shoulder. It turned instantly into a mountain of flint. They stopped near the mountain, and took a rest. They also had a meal, and, attaching fresh reindeer, started on again. Cu'mo came to the mountain and gnawed it. Chips of flint flew in every direction. He gnawed it through and went across it, kettle and all.

The second sister said to the other, "O sister! Put your ear to the ground and try to hear whether he is following us again?" They listened, and, lo! The kettle was rattling quite close behind. Then the oldest sister took out a piece of steel from a strike-a-light. She said to the steel, "O steel! You were part of a strike-a-light and produced fire. Now turn into a river of fire from earth to heaven, from east to west." Then she threw the steel back over her shoulder, and it turned into a river of fire, from earth to heaven, from east to west. Cu'mo came to that river and tried to cross it, but he was confused by the fire and perished there. "Ah," he called after the sisters, "you ran away from me; but nevertheless my mother will catch you." The sisters were hurrying on. All the reindeer fell and perished from exhaustion. The sisters sped onward on foot. At last they came to a river. It was quite deep, and there was no fjord, so that they could not cross it. On the other side of the river sat an old woman scraping a skin. "Oh, grand-mother! Help us to cross the river!" "Ah, you dogs! Cross it by your own skill." "O grandmother! We cannot. Do help us!" The old woman stretched one of her legs across the river like a bridge, and they crossed over on it. "Where do you come from?" asked the old woman. "We ran away from Cu'mo. He wanted to eat us, but we burned him in a river of fire." "O, you dogs! Cu'mo is my only son. I shall punish you for it." So she locked them in an empty storehouse, and hurried to help Cu'mo.

(After this follows the well-known episode detailing how the Fox saved the girls from the She-Monster, leaving in their stead

clothes filled with twigs and ashes to be swallowed by the Monster. The narrator, however, declared that she had forgotten the details, and left the tale unfinished.)

Told by Anne Vastriakoff, a Russianized Yukaghir woman, in the village Omolon at the confluence of the Omolon River with the Kolyma River, in the autumn of 1896.

9. *Yukaghir Tale.*

There was a man and his wife. They had a little boy. One time the woman felt a yearning for some pike. Her mouth watered at the thought of it. Then she said to her husband, "Do go to the lake and set your nets! I want some pike to eat." He went to the lake, and on the same day he caught a large pike. The woman immediately cooked it. She ate the fish beginning at the intestine and ate as far as the head. When she came to the mouth and opened the teeth, she saw that they were of iron. She was scared, and threw away what was left of the pike; but from that time on she grew with child, and after due time gave birth to a girl. The girl grew up rapidly, not like an ordinary child from year to year, but hourly; so that on the next day she was playing out of doors with her brother, who, although older, was nevertheless much smaller than she. In playing, she said, "one day more, or perhaps two days, and I shall eat all of you." The boy went to his father and mother and told them of her words; but they did not believe him, and even punished him. "You do not like your sister, and therefore you slander her." The same happened in the evening and again the next morning. The boy could not stand it any longer. He felt angry, frightened, and sore. So he left his parents and fled. Far away in the tundra he saw a house with an outer room. He entered there. Two wolves and two bears were tied up in front of the inner door. The animals wanted to attack him; but he whistled three times, and they grew quiet and lay down. Then he entered the inner room. In the middle a white reindeer skin was spread. On the skin slept a naked girl, dazzling white of body. Her tresses were auburn and as long as the sleeve of an overcoat. He hid under her tresses and slept with the girl. In due time she awoke, sniffed about, and said, "who are you? Make yourself visible. If you are an old man, I will have you for a father; if a young man, I will take you for a husband." So he appeared from under her tresses. She married him, and they lived together. After some time he wanted to visit his father and mother; so he asked his wife to give him some animal to drive, even if it were a wolf or a bear. She gave him a reindeer with six legs. He set off. When near the house of his parents, he tied the reindeer to a tree and went on foot. Then he arrived at the house and opened the door. The Pike-Girl had eaten up my father and mother long before, and was playing with the bare skulls. As soon as she saw him, she threw the skulls under the bed. The young man felt afraid. She rushed up to him, however, and said, "O brother dear! You have come at last." In the evening she asked him, "where are you going to sleep?" He said, "I am going to sleep on the roof." "Why do you do so?" said the girl, "I do not want to sleep alone. I have not seen you for such a long time." "Well, then," said the brother, "I will lie down close to the chimney-hole, and will thrust my legs down the chimney-hole, so that you may look at them, when going to sleep." He did just so, and feigned sleep. The girl tried to catch at the legs, but the chimney was too narrow; and feeling tired, she desisted. After a while she was snoring. Then with great caution he left the roof and went away. He found his reindeer and raced off.

He drove the whole night through, then he looked back and saw that the pike girl was following in pursuit. He urged on the reindeer and it galloped off; but the Pike-Girl galloped still faster, just like a winged bird. After a while she overtook the reindeer, and at first tore off one of its extra legs. While she was eating that leg, the reindeer hurried on. She finished the leg, and again gave pursuit. This time she tore off the other extra leg. The reindeer galloped off with four legs. Then she overtook it again, and tore off one leg more. Then the reindeer could run no longer so the young man left it and hurried on afoot. He had one blunt arrow. Holding this, he ran onward. When the Pike-Girl had eaten the reindeer leg she gave pursuit again. When she was close to him, he lifted up the arrow and said, "There, arrow mine! You were an arrow. Now turn into an iron tree. I want to be safe on top of that tree." Instantly, it turned into a big iron tree, and he was high up on its top. The tree was as thick through as a man can embrace. The Pike-Girl came to the tree, and said, "O brother mine! Your iron tree is not tempered, but my iron teeth are tempered and hard." So she gnawed at the tree, and iron splinters flew around like rotten wood. A jay flew by, and he said to it:

O jay! Fly to my wife!
Bid her send off her dogs!

But the jay answered with a man's voice, "I will not fly. When you were living with your father and mother, whenever I came to your drying poles and wanted to peck at the pike-roe, your blunt arrow would instantly hiss by close to my head. I will not fly." A snow-bunting flew by, and he said to it:

O, snow-bunting! Fly to my wife,
And bid her send off her dogs!

So the bunting flew away and came to his wife's house. It perched upon the window-sill, and twittered:

Pititi pititi,
Send off the dogs!

She heard this, and in a moment she sent off two wolves and two bears. They ran off and reached the tree. The Pike-Girl, as soon as she saw them, turned into an ermine and went under the roots of the tree. The bears dug at the roots to get at the ermine, and at last caught it. The young man descended from the tree with his ax and chopped up the ermine. He gathered the pieces and burnt them in the fire, and the ashes he let fly to the winds. Then he went back to his wife and told her all. After that they lived in peace, and they are still living. The end.

Told by Anne Korkin, a Russianized Yukaghir woman, in the village of Sukhamoye in the Kolyma country, in the autumn of 1896.

10. The She-Monster.

There lived a family. They had three daughters and no sons. After some time the father and the mother died. The girls remained alone. They hunted game and caught fish, and in the summer time picked berries and gathered roots. They never knew a man. One time the eldest sister stayed at home. The other two went berrying. They came home. The youngest wanted to be petted: so she dropped into the other sister's lap, and said,

"O, my sister! I am so very hungry! Give me something to eat." The eldest sister, standing by, said, "why, then go to the storehouse, and pick out a piece of the very best dried fish. That is the food for you." Then she laughed. The youngest sister looked up at her, and saw pieces of raw meat sticking out all around between her teeth. She felt frightened, and whispered to her second sister, "Why, sister, look about! All our stores of dried meat, reindeer, and elk, are gone! And why are the teeth of our eldest sister filled with pieces of meat?" The second sister refused to believe it; and, still, she also was afraid to look up, lest she should see those horrible teeth. After a few days the two younger sisters went for a visit to the graves of their parents. They invited the eldest one to go with them, but she refused. They arrived at the graves, and found that they had been dug open. The body of the father had been eaten up, and of the body of the mother only a part was left. This was the doing of their eldest sister. They sorrowed and cried aloud. Then they went back, and on the way they talked to each other. "O, sister! We cannot go home. She will finish eating our mother, then she will come for us. Let us rather leave in time! Let us run to the open country, or let us flee across the blue sea!" Just then they saw on high a flock of wild geese flying. They shouted upward to the geese, "O geese! Drop down to us a feather apiece!" The geese, ever so many, dropped down for them a feather apiece. The girls gathered the feathers and stuck them between their fingers. Then they flew up, and followed the geese. The youngest sister said to the second one, "O sister dear! She will doubtless pursue us. Take care, though, if she should call to you, and shout, and ask for an answer, not to take any heed! And especially do not look back at her."

Then the eldest sister actually went in pursuit. They flew on high, she ran below on the ground, and cried out, "O sisters dear! Why have you forsaken me? Have we not been nursed at the same mother's breast? Have we not been begotten in the same mother's womb? And now you leave me behind! How shall I live alone, without your company?" The second sister was moved with compassion: so she looked back and down. In a moment the She-Monster opened her mouth, and the girl fell directly into it. The She-Monster swallowed her without chewing. The youngest sister flew on, and did not look back, notwithstanding all her cries and entreaties. She flew onward; the eldest sister ran in pursuit. At last the

She-Monster gave up, and at the last only shouted, "This time you do not want to look at me! But later you will be married, and you will have a boy and a girl. The girl will sit on an earth bench,[22] and she will play with her little scissors; and the boy will play with his bow and arrows. Then I shall come to you." The other one flew on. At last she saw a small house, standing all alone. She sat down near the chimney-hole, and looked down through the chimney. A young man was sitting near the fireplace, feathering his arrows. He did this for some time. Then he was lacking a white feather for the last arrow. So he said, "Oh, I wish I had one more feather!" In a moment she tore away one of her feathers and let it drop through the chimney. He caught it, and looked up, but no one was there. So he finished the arrow, and brought some more arrows and feathers, and resumed the feathering. After a while he was again lacking one feather for the last arrow. This time it was a black feather. "Oh," said he, "I wish I had one more feather." And immediately she let drop a black feather. After that she dropped a third feather. Then he said, "who are you? If you are really human, come down and let me look at you, and if you are an evil spirit, then remain invisible." She took off her feathers and turned into her former self. Then she descended into the house. He took her for a wife.

They lived together for a long time, and she brought forth, first a boy, then a girl. The husband went out every day to go in search of game.

The children were growing up. One spring day they were playing on the earth bench in front of the house. Then suddenly appeared her eldest sister, the She-Monster. She hugged the children and kissed them. In doing this she bit off the upper lip of the boy and the under lip of the girl. They shrieked, and ran to their mother. Their faces were covered with blood. O, she became so frightened! "Who has been treating you like this? Or perhaps you have been fighting with others?" "Oh, no! It was our aunt, who kissed us." Then the eldest sister entered. They did not even salute each other. Then the human sister wanted to go out. "Do not do that," said the Monster. "But I want to ease myself." "All right! But make the utmost haste. Hardly step out of the house before you are back again." She sat down near the fireplace and waited for her. The human sister went out of the house, and the boy slipped out after her. They ran to one of their storehouses. Standing there was an old wooden box. They squeezed themselves into this box. Then the woman said, "O, wooden box! Henceforth be an iron storehouse standing high upon twelve iron supports."[23] The wooden box turned into an iron storehouse with twelve supports, and they were safe within. The boy called for his father, and she called for her husband. The eldest sister went out and saw the girl: so she caught her and swallowed her. Merely the feet stuck out from her mouth. After a while, she spit out her small bones. She came to the iron storehouse and gnawed at the supports, and splinters of iron flew in all directions. Then the iron storehouse rocked to and fro, with only three supports left. All of a sudden the man came up. He struck the She-Monster with his sword and killed her. He chopped her into small pieces and burned her in the fire. She was burning, and every kind of worms and vermin crawled out of her body. He gathered them all, scraped them up with a shovel, and thrust them back into the fire. At last her body was destroyed, and he threw the ashes to all four winds. The remaining bones he threw into the sea. Then they went to another country. They lived there.

Told by Katherine Rumiantzev, a Russianized Yukaghir woman, in the village of Pokhotsk, in the Kolyma country, summer of 1896.

11. The Monster with Iron Teeth.

There were three brothers. One time they traveled together in lonely places. The first night they stopped at a way house. They made a fire, cooked some bread-soup, and had supper. While they were eating, a board of the floor was lifted up. There appeared a monster with iron teeth, two feet long. The eldest brother said to the other two, "go out and get the dogs and sledges ready. I will stay here. And you must wait outside for me." They took their bread-soup[24] and went out of the house. They could hear the eldest brother within fighting with the monster. They did not know in what way, but could only hear great noise and gnashing of teeth. Before sunrise their brother came out of the house. They started off on their sledges. They drove till dark. Then they saw another log cabin. They entered, made a fire, and prepared some soup. As soon as they had swallowed a spoonful or two, a board was lifted in one of the front corners of the house and up came the Monster with Iron Teeth.[25] The oldest brother made the other two go out and he fought the monster alone. The next morning, when he came out, they saw that he had turned into a quite different being. All his blood, and his face, were no longer human. He was more like a devil. The second brother said to the youngest one, "Look at him! He has iron teeth at least half a foot long."

They drove onward again until evening. It had grown quite dark when they came to another log cabin. They made a fire and prepared soup. When they were half through with their meal, there appeared a woman with iron teeth, covered with blood, who rushed at them. The eldest brother also fought the woman. The other two exchanged looks, and slipped out of doors. Then they turned their sledges back and drove homeward. They traveled the whole night and the next day. Then they came to the log cabin in which the second fight with the Monster of Iron Teeth had taken place. They made a fire and prepared their soup. Then they heard outside the shuffling of snowshoes. They were so much frightened, that neither dared to go out. Then the door opened of itself, and the oldest brother entered. He was very angry. "Why are you making so much trouble for me? If you want to leave me behind, why do you stop in this very place?" He had hardly finished these words, when the Monster with Iron Teeth appeared. They fought again; and the eldest brother said, "Go away! Do not wait for me any longer! But mind you do not stop at the first log cabin. When I am through with this fight, I shall give chase; and if I catch you in the first log cabin, I shall fight the first monster, but I shall also punish you."

They drove away from there, crying for fear. They traveled throughout the night and the next day. After sunset they came to the log cabin, and of course wanted to pass it, but they could not induce their dogs to pass by. All the dogs rushed in and fought as if they were worrying somebody to death. No one was to be seen, however. They wrangled with the dogs far into the evening, and at last dragged them out of the house. They were quite tired and hungry; and the second brother at last proposed, "Let us stay here over night!" The youngest answered, "how could we do that? The monster will appear, and then our brother; and he warned us beforehand that he will punish us." The second brother answered, "Excuse him for a fool! I do not fear him at all. I myself have become as bad as he." The youngest brother looked up, and saw that the second brother also had iron teeth half a foot long. He was so badly frightened that he could not speak. Meanwhile the shuffling of snowshoes was heard outside, and there entered a being similar to their brother in face and body; but they did not recognize him. He said not a single word, but rushed at the second brother. They fought like wolves. The youngest brother slipped outside, took his dogs, and fled. He drove on until midnight, and heard nothing. After midnight, however, he heard a voice like a distant shaman's call. The voice said, "a man is pursuing his own brother. He wants to gnaw at his bones, to eat of his meat, to drink of his blood!" The youngest brother out of fright, urged his dogs on with all his might. In the meantime he said to himself, "when he overtakes me, how shall I defend myself?" He remembered having heard from older people, that, when pursued by a monster, one may defend oneself by striking the monster with an old kettle. Then the monster will fall down and will be unable to follow for a couple of hours, which at least will give respite at the most critical moment. So he loosened the kettle, and made ready for the blow.

Kettle in hand, he watched when the monster should reach the sledge. When it was at hand, he uttered an incantation and struck its face with the blackened kettle. The monster fell face down, and cried aloud, "Oh, you are too clever for me! I shall catch you, nevertheless. The village is yet far off. I shall rest for a couple of hours; then I shall catch you, drink of your blood, eat of your meat and gnaw your bones." The other one urged his dogs to the limit of their strength. He knew, that the village was not very far away. They moved on. The monster gave pursuit again. Then they heard the bell in the church belfry ringing. He crossed himself, and said, "Thank God, I am safe now!" And the monster shouted from behind, "you are safe; but I shall catch you somewhere in time to come." The young man reached the village, and straightway went to the priest. He said that in such and such places in the woods there were monsters; that these monsters were probably unburied corpses, which walk abroad and attack human beings. The priest listened to him, and then laid a curse of the Church upon the monsters; that they should cease to appear and make trouble. After that all the people traveled about without fear or danger, and they met with nothing extraordinary. The end.

Told by Nicholas Kusakoff, a Russian Creole (cossack), at the village of Pokhotsk in the Kolyma country, summer of 1896.

12. The Girl from the Grave-Box.

Some Lamut were living in three tents. One of them had two sons. They had set their deadfalls at distant places: so the father sent his sons to visit these traps. They came to the traps and walked along all day. They stopped for the night at the farthest traps. Then the elder brother said to the younger one, "Oh, I wish we could find here some girl to be our assistant! It is tedious work to cut firewood and cook food. Have we not enough to do with the traps?" "Do not say so!" said the younger brother. "Why do you wish for a girl? We are in the wilderness. If anybody comes, it will be some monster or spirit." The first brother replied, "be it who it may, I should like to have a girl for an assistant." In the middle of the night a girl came, handsome, like the sunrise. The older brother took her for his wife. When day was coming, she went away, but the next evening she came again. They lived in this manner.

A week passed. Then the younger brother said in the morning, "how long shall we remain here? Our father and mother must be anxious on our behalf." But the other one refused to listen. He said, "you may go home, but I shall stay here." The younger brother went home on his snowshoes, and told his parents what had happened. His father called together several neighbors, all men, and they went to bring the young man. He refused to come and cried for vexation; but they bound him hand and foot, tied him to a reindeer-sledge, and took him home. The father said, "now, I shall stay and see who lived with him, a human being or some impure creature." So he remained there for a night, made a fire, and waited. After sunset the girl came. When she saw that another man was in the house, she wailed aloud, and went back into the heart of the woods. She was wailing all the way back, till at last her voice died out. Next morning the father followed in her tracks. He came to a small river, which he followed upstream. At last he found on the bank an ancient wooden grave-box.[26] The tracks of the girl led to that grave-box, and then vanished. The old man opened the box and saw a skeleton. The bones held together only by the dry sinew.

He cut the skeleton, disjointed all the bones, and laid them down in four separate places.

After that the young man began to droop and pine and suffer. When walking, he would even stumble over the grass. When near to death, he said, "as you have done to my love, so do also to me." So they took his body to the grave-box, gathered the bones of the girl together, and laid him by their side. After that they left the country and went far off. The end.

Told by Katherine Rumiantzev, a Russianized Yukaghir woman, at the village of Pokhotsk in the lower Kolyma country, summer of 1896.

13. Small-Pox, a Yukaghir Tale. (First Version)

There lived a man all by himself. One time a woman came to him. She was Small-Pox. She was quite tall and lean of body, her teeth were long and sharp, and her eyes burned like glowing coals. "Where are the other people?" asked Small-Pox. "I do not know." "How is it that you do not know? Are you not human-born? Where are your house and village mates?" "No," said the man, "as long ago as I can remember, I always lived all alone." Small-Pox stayed with him. Every morning and every evening she climbed a very high tree and listened in every direction. One time she descended, and said, "yonder to the east, I can hear early in the morning and late in the evening the ringing of iron;" and indeed, there were young men chopping wood, and young girls carrying water from the river in iron pails. For this reason, even at present, our old men forbid young men and girls to chop wood and to carry water early in the morning or late in the evening. Every one must prepare the wood and bring the daily store of water in broad daylight.

"Oh!" said Small-Pox, "human people are living on that side. You must carry me to those people." "And how shall I carry you to them? Here is a bladder of the ptarmigan. Creep into it. I will carry you concealed in the bladder." She entered the bladder which he tied up with a cord, and then hung it up before the fireplace to dry. The bladder was drying up more and more, and she was drying with it. Day and night she struggled within the bladder, but by no means could she pierce it and come out. After a while she became quite shrivelled up, mere bones and dried skin; and even her voice was hardly audible.

"Oh, let me go!" pleaded Small-Pox in a hoarse whisper. "I promise I will never touch any man whatever of your house and kin." "And how will you recognize my house and kin?" "Let the people of your house and kin wear small red tufts on their caps." For this reason the Yukaghir people of our clan wear red tufts on their caps even at the present time.

Then the man opened the bladder and took out Small-Pox. She was so weak that she could not stand up, a mere soul without a body. He put her on a board and sent it floating down the river. "Go wherever you choose! Land wherever you may!"

Told by Nicholas Vostriakoft, the head man of the Vostriakoft clan of the Russianized Yukaghir in the village Omolon, at the confluence of the Omolon and Kolyma rivers, summer of 1896.

(Second Version.)

There was a large Yukaghir village on the Indighirka River. In that village lived a powerful shaman. One time he beat the drum; then he went out of the house and said, "a great disease is coming towards us, the like of which we have never seen." There was a crossway where three small trails converged into a single one which was very broad and straight. He went to the crossway and hid under the roots of a large tree. Lying there, he listened for those whose approach he had foreseen. Three sisters were coming along the road. They were riding red horses, their coats were as red as fire, and their hair was burning like lightning. The younger sisters were inquiring of the oldest one, "where shall we go this time?" The eldest sister answered, "this time go on without me. Nearby there is a large Yukaghir village. A powerful shaman lives there. I want to take him away." "Do not speak so loud!" answered the other sister, "somebody may overhear you." "Who should overhear me? Deep woods are all around us." The shaman, however, was hidden under the roots of a tree, and heard all. He ran home, and said to his house people, "get the meal ready.

At mealtime she will come to the people eating food." He had a magic iron box, sealed with a magic seal. He opened it and put it upon the table, close to himself. They ate, and during the meal a long red hair fell upon the table, at the left hand side of the shaman. All at once he caught the hair and put it into the box. He closed it and sealed it up with the magic seal. "Now make a big fire," said he to the people. They made a big fire, and he put the box into it, and began to rake the fire. Soon the box was glowing red. Then a wail, like that of a human voice was heard from the box. "Oh, set me free! I cannot stand it." "Ah, you cannot!" said the shaman, and raked the fire. Thus, he roasted her for three days and three nights. On the fourth day there was a faint squeal like the voice of a red fox. "Oh, please let me go! I cannot stand it." Then he asked the other people of the village, "what shall I do to her? Shall I really set her free?" "You are the shaman," said the people, "do what you think best. We cannot tell." "All right," said the shaman, "let me have a look at her." He opened the box. A red girl was sitting within it, half dead with exhaustion, mere skin and bones, dryer than a withered leaf. "Now you may go," said the shaman, "but be sure not to forget our treatment of you." "I shall not forget. But I am very weary, I cannot walk. Give me some food and a drink of water." So he kept her for three days, and gave her food and water. After that she grew a little stronger; so she went to the woods, found her own horse, and hurried off. When departing, she swore to herself that she would never go back to that awful place. So she came to the crossway. Her sisters had been waiting for her for two days. "Where have you been so long?" "Oh, the Yukaghir shaman caught me and nearly murdered me. He put me into a box and burned me in the fire." "There you are! Did we not warn you not to be so loud in your boasting lest somebody should overhear you?" "You did. And where have you been?" "Oh, we have had some little fun. We slew the people of one village, and in another we left only one boy and one girl." After that the sisters rode on.

Told by Timothy, a Tunguso-Yukaghir, on the western tundra of the Kolyma, spring of 1895.

14. Tale of a Shaman.

A shaman was living with some other people. One time he took his drum and began to practise. Then he died suddenly. Now, the ancient Yakut had the following custom: Whenever a man of importance died, every one would leave the village, and move to another place. So the people went away. The shaman was left in an empty hut, stone dead, drum in hand. In midwinter, on the twelfth day after the shortest day, the young men of the Yakut were in the habit of gathering and playing games. One young man suddenly said, "why, comrades, who dares to go to the dead shaman and cut off his braid? He must bring it here as proof that he has been there." The others said, "who will go? That is too much to ask; and, by the way, at what time of day do you want us to go?" "To be sure, about midnight, in utter darkness." "We shall not go. Better go yourself." "I should go on a good wager. Then I should cut off his braid and bring it here."

They argued among themselves. The one said, "Let us bet a horse each!" They consented, but secretly they proposed to send a man along. This man was to lie down behind the shaman; and when the daring one should stretch out his hand for the braid, the other one was to make a noise and clatter, and so frighten him off. Then the one asked, "is it time to go?" They said, "all right, go!" and he rode off. He arrived at the empty hut, tied his horse to the post, and entered the hut. When he was opening the door, he heard in the darkness a ringing of iron and a clattering of the drum, as if the shaman were stirring about; but he said, "there, uncle, you may ring and clatter, but I shall take that for which I came." So he approached the dead body, and, catching hold of the braid, cut it off at the very roots. Then he went out. Behind him something rang and clattered again, but he paid no attention to it. He came to his companions and showed them the braid; the other man arrived later, and said, "indeed, he is quite undaunted. I made a noise and beat the drum, but he paid no heed at all. He cut away the braid and carried it off." So that man won the wager, a horse from each of the partners. That is all.

Told by John Parin, a Russianized Yakut, in the village of Bystraia, in the Kolyma country, summer of 1896.

15. Tale of a Shaman.

There was the head man of a village. I do not know exactly whether it was a village of Yukaghir or of the Yakut clan. This head man used to gather tribute among his clansmen. Then he carried it southward to the town of Yakutsk on the river Aldan.[27] On the Aldan lived the tribute chief of their tribe. One time this Kolyma head man came to the Aldan tribute chief.[28] The wife of the latter was suffering very much from one day to the next and they were afraid she might die. The Kolyma head man, seeing her condition said to the tribute chief, "have no care about my dinner, I will go elsewhere."The tribute chief answered, "you were my guest in times of good fortune. Will you go away in these evil hours?" So the Kolyma head man entered, and saw sitting there in the house around a table, seven people, all quite unknown to him. He asked the tribute chief, "who are these people, your workmen or your guests?" Oh!" said the tribute chief, "what are you thinking of! These people are no workmen, nor are they simple guests. They are shamans, all seven of them. They have come here for nine days, and they practise their art all the while;

but we do not see any help. My wife is getting worse and worse. O friend! Your Kolyma country is renowned for its shamans and magicians; and you too, come from a country far distant, and you select your assistant from the whole community without doubt with great care. I am sure that you pay attention to this (ie,to magic). Can you not ask your assistant? Perhaps he knows enough to get for us at least temporary relief, even if for only a couple of hours." "I cannot tell. Indeed, as a young man, he suffered from fits, and perhaps he really is able to practise the art of shamanism, though I do not know whether for himself only or also on behalf of other people. However, we may call him here, and see what he can do. Where is he? Go and call him."

They brought the assistant. He was a small fellow, quite young, with only one eye. The house master asked him, "here, you, of Kolyma birth, perhaps you have some knowledge of this matter, some shamanistic power or magical force. Have a look at my wife, and try to help her somehow!" "All right!" said the fellow. "If I were in my own place, or if I had at least my own shamanistic garment, I might try to do something." To this the tribute chief answered, "if you only will try, I will procure the necessary garment and all appurtenances."The man was silent for a while. Then he said, "I will try to practise, as far as I may and know. But if she should die, do not be angry with me!" "Oh, no! Surely not! Do whatever you like. Before the beginning, however, give me a few hours only. Let me have one more look at her, though she is suffering." They brought the shamanistic garment and arrayed him in it. The garment was too large for him. He looked in it just like a stump in an overcoat. The owner of the garment said, "tie him up with a girdle. He will tear off all the tassels." One man went up to him and said, "Let me gird you up!" "Wait a while," said the Kolyma shaman, "then you may gird me. I will give you a signal."[29] So he began to practise. He croaked three times like a raven; then he roared three times like a bear; then he howled three times like a wolf. After that he stood up. His head pierced the roof, and the garment burst between the shoulders. Then the door flew open, and the seven shamans were hurled out of the house like seven shreds of skin. They died on the spot. He began to practise. After some time he went to the patient, and cut her body into small pieces. Each piece he took into his hands and put into his mouth, sucked it all around, and then blew on it. He put them together, and blew upon them three times. They joined again, and were covered with a new skin. He blew three times more, and the body breathed. After that he stepped toward the entrance and sang for an hour, then for another hour. At the beginning of the third hour, the woman came to herself, and turned over on the other side. She even asked for a little piece of meat to be put into her mouth. So he went back to her from the door, and asked her, "how do you feel?" "I feel numb all over!" He resumed his singing and performed until dawn. Then he stopped and ordered all the people to lie down to sleep. When they awoke, the woman awoke with them, and asked for food and drink. They put another piece of meat into her mouth. From this time on she recovered rapidly, and after three days she was able to take food and drink without assistance.

After that the tribute chief took his best horse, renowned in that region for its swiftness. He put on it a saddle of silver, a bridle of steel inlaid with silver, and a saddle cloth embroidered with silk. To the saddle he tied a pouch containing two hundred rubles in cash. Then he took the horse to the Kolyma shaman, but the shaman refused to accept anything. So the tribute chief felt greatly afraid, and with much insistence and almost in tears, begged him to take something. At last, the shaman consented. He took the horse; but the bridle and the saddle, together with the saddle cloth, he took off and gave them back to the master. He took thirty rubles only, and those not in silver, but in paper money. He rolled them up and tucked them into the horse's left ear. Then he blew upon the horse and struck it with his staff; and the horse soared up on high, flew away, and vanished. They asked him, "where did you send it?" "I sent it to my mother and sister. This will last them until my return."

Told by Nicholas Kusakoff, a Russian Creole, in the village of the Pokhotsk, in the Kolyma country, summer of 1896.

16. A Hunting Tale.[30]

Three men lived together. I cannot tell to what tribe or clan they may have belonged, whether they were peasants or cossacks, or Yakut or Yukaghir or something else. They were good hunters, and every fall with the first snow they would set off to hunt sable and red and gray foxes. Each time they would divide the skins into three equal parts. One year the snow fell very early and it was time to go on the hunt. One of the companions, who was somewhat poorer than the rest went to the others and invited them to go. It seems that he wanted to buy some provisions, and so wanted to make haste to get the means for purchasing them. The other, being richer, wanted to wait a couple of days. He waited two days, but still they were not ready. They asked him to wait a little longer. He waited again. Meantime the fallen snow had grown harder. It was the very time to go: so he went to his companions, and said, "See here! Perhaps you are not yet ready, but I shall not wait any longer. You see, the snow has already hardened. We have missed the last time. Further delay will spoil the hunt altogether."

So he went home, mounted his horse, and called his hunting dog! With these he went, and at once found the tracks of four sables. He had a good dog: so he let him loose, and the dog followed the sables and chased them to an open lake. There on the ice he caught all four of them. He crossed over the lake, and on the other shore made a fire, prepared some food, and skinned the sables. All at once the other two companions arrived and congratulated him on the successful hunt. He thanked them, invited them to pass the night with him, and the next morning to start hunting in common, as was their custom in former times. They consented, and stayed there. The night passed. In the morning they got up and went hunting in different directions. They also chose the halting-place for the next night, and promised to be there in time for the evening meal. The first hunter arrived there, however, the last of all, he was so late. The other two brought eight sables, and he alone also brought eight. They skinned them all and dried the skins. The next morning they proposed to continue the hunt; but the first hunter said, "I must go home for a couple of days. We will divide these skins equally among us; then I will go home, and be back in two or three days." They had, in all, twenty sable skins, but in distributing them they gave him only five skins, and took fifteen for themselves, and he was the one who had caught more than half of the whole. So he said, "no, that is not fair. Let us share equally. You have given me too little. We must have six sables a piece, and the two sables over are surplus." They refused to comply, and offered him the former five. He took these five skins and felt wronged:

so he departed without any greeting. After some hesitation, they followed him. They rode quite silently for a long time, and then they saw near the trail a house that they had never seen before. Near the entrance stood a birch tree, very thin and high. They wondered at the house and the tree, and asked themselves, "how is it that never before have we seen this house in our neighborhood? Let us enter and see who may live in it!" So they entered, and saw an old man, quite small, and wizened with age. He was so thin that his head was held in place by a single sinew only. His arms and legs were like grass blades, almost ready to break in two. They entered, and saluted the old man. He said, "sit down, O hunters! Tell me, please, what success have you had in your pursuit?" The two said, "thank God! Fair enough." The third one replied, "Look here, Uncle! We hunted together, and were indeed fairly successful. I caught a little more than they, and in the end they refused to give me even a fair and equal share." "How was that," asked the old man. He told what had happened. "Listen, my friends!" said the old man. "I will tell you a story of a similar kind. I too, in my time, was a hunter, and was always ready to wander about. No kind of game could escape me, but in sharing with my companions, I was too exacting and close-fisted. One time, while traveling alone, I met a young woman, or rather a girl. She came to me and stretched out her hand and gave me a blow on the ear. At the same time she said, "you were a man, now you must be a wolf. For three days, you shall run, and after the third day you shall come here to this very place." So I, who had been a man, immediately turned into a wolf. I ran about for three whole days, and then I returned to the same place from which I had started. The woman was already there. She struck me again on the face, and said aloud, "You were a wolf, now turn into a man again!" I turned into a man. She took my hand and led me on to a village. When we were near the village, she struck me again on the face, and said, "you were a man, now turn into a bunch of grass." So I turned into a bunch of grass and remained motionless at the place where I stood, close to the trail. The people of that village were driving over me, and the runners of the sledges hurt me every time. The people often felt angry at me, and wanted to cut me down, but they neglected to do so. Well, I existed somehow. I felt much pain and fear, and it was only in the depths of the night that I had any respite at all. I cannot tell how long I stayed there, days or months, or maybe years. I was more dead than alive. Then at last the woman came. She kicked me, and said aloud, "You were a bunch of grass, now turn again into a man!" So I turned into a man. I felt quite savage, and wanted to retaliate. She took my hand and led me on. I said to myself, "what if I try and do the same to her?" So I stretched out my hand and gave her a blow on the ear, and said aloud, "you were a woman, now you must turn into a birch tree." I remembered the incantation; but in my haste I could not think of anything besides a birch tree, so she turned into a birch tree. From that time on, she has been a tree, and I do not know how to restore her to her former human shape. The second part of the incantation has ceased to work. I have tried it again and again; but it has lost its force, I do not know why. So I constructed this small house, and am living here. I say to myself, "Let me die at least near this birch tree! So you see I am severely punished. My arms and legs have become like grass blades, my body is almost ready to break down, and my head to fall off. I think that God has sent this punishment to me and to the woman, in order to make us a living lesson to other people who pass by on this road. So I say to you two, cease to do wrong to your companion, lest worse luck befall you!"

The two greedy ones felt afraid, and they said, "the old man speaks the truth, it is too dangerous." They shared the sable skins equally, and gave six skins to the first hunter. Two sable skins were left over. They took one for themselves, and gave the other to the first hunter. Then the old man fell down and died, and the birch tree turned into its former self and became a woman. "Who are you?" asked the men. "I am hunting luck," said the woman. She asked them to help her in burying the old man. The other two hunters refused to do so; but the first hunter said, "I will bury him all alone." So he dug the grave, and then made a coffin of larch-wood. He buried him in due form, as is the custom. The woman thanked him; and when he departed, she gave him a small pouch made of various shreds of cloth. He took the pouch, and said to himself, "for what is this pouch? It seems of no use." She answered his thoughts, "do not say that this pouch is of no use. It will be good all your life." He went home and opened the pouch. It was full of silver money. He spent the money, but whenever he took out money, the pouch was filled again. So he lived and lived, and could not empty the pouch, and his widow after him also could not spend all the money.

Told by Nicholas Kusakoff, a Russian Creole, in the village of Pokhotsk, in the Kolyma country, summer of 1896.

17. Story about the Bad Merchant.[31]

Three brothers lived. I cannot tell who they were, whether Russian or Yakut. They lived in a wild place, somewhat after the manner of Lamut nomads. Two of the brothers used to go on hunting trips. The third one stayed at home. None of them knew whether they ever had had father, mother, or sister, or even so much as a relative. The two elder brothers would come home for a day or two, and then leave again for six or seven days. They used to bring home costly peltries, also reindeer and elk carcasses. They gave everything to the third brother, and they did not even care what happened to their game. They never asked him, "what are you doing with all these things? Do you store them away, or simply throw them away as rubbish?"

One day these two brothers prepared for a longer trip than usual. So they said to the housekeeping brother, "perhaps we shall not be back for a long time. Stay at home, and eat of the meat we have brought." After that they left. One evening, the brother who kept house was singing songs for his own recreation. Then he heard a noise without. He hurried to the entrance; but at this moment entered a man, tall of stature, carrying in his hands a bear lance inlaid with silver. He was clad in beautiful garments embroidered with silk. It was the bad merchant. The young man was much frightened, and receded to a remote comer; but the visitor said gruffly, "Help my workman unload the pack-horses!" The house master hurried out, and saw a man busying himself with nine pack-horses. He helped him take off the loads. While doing this, he heard somebody cough. He looked back, and saw a woman wrapped up in fox garments. He approached her, and asked her with much gentleness to enter the house. Then he opened the door and showed her the way. As soon as she was inside, he helped her lay off her garments. She was middle-aged, but very strong and pretty. The Bad Merchant looked at his doings with much scorn. He sat before the fire, warming his back. All the time he held in his hands the big bear lance inlaid with silver.

After a while the Bad Merchant asked the house master with still more gruffness, "do you not know of some good pasture here for horses?" "Yes, I know of one." "Then help my workman to take the horses there." They had a meal and drank their tea. After that they took the horses to the pasture. When they were going back, the house master asked of the workman, "and who are you, this visitor and the woman?" "Do you not know him? He is the Bad Merchant. I thought he would kill you at first sight. He has a very bad temper. No house did he ever pass that he did not kill somebody. It is your special luck that you have been spared so far." The young man ceased asking, and kept his thoughts to himself. They entered the house. The Bad Merchant was sitting, as before, near the fire, lance in hand. The house master hurried to his back room and threw out a great number of furs, sables, gray foxes, black foxes, bears, all kinds of peltries that exist in the world. He threw all this at the feet of the Merchant. The latter, seeing such riches, put the lance on the floor and bent over the heap. The young man, with an innocent face, picked up the lance. "What a beautiful lance!" said he, "and what a shaft! Strong like iron. Even against a bear such a shaft would hold out and never break." Then he poised it in his hands. Together with the shaft it weighed no less than one pound. He took the lance by the iron and lifted it, shaft upward, and all at once struck the Bad Merchant on the neck. The woman seized a knife and tried to stab him; but he struck her with the shaft, and she fell down senseless. Then he cried to the workman, "Bring those elk-hide laying there in the corner!" With them he bound him securely. The woman came to herself, but he violated her. Then he said to the workman, "you accompanied him on his travel, and were compelled by him to do his work, and he paid you with blows. You might have expected a violent death at almost any hour. Now that God has brought you here to me, I restore you to freedom. Take his horses and go wherever you wish!" The workman stayed there, however, for five days more. After that the elder brothers came, and saw the Bad Merchant in bonds. The woman was bound likewise. So the elder brothers said, "Ah! It is you! We have heard much about you. So many people of these parts complain of your doings. This time God has given us occasion to overcome you. Now the complaints of the people will cease." They turned to their brother and thanked him heartily: "it is you who caught him and liberated the country." I do not know, however, what they did to the prisoners. Probably they tortured them to death. That is all.

Told by Nicholas Kusakoff, a Russian Creole, in the village of Pokhotsk, in the Kolyma country, summer of 1895.

18. Stepmother and Stepdaughter.[32]

There was an old man with his wife. They had one daughter. After some time the old woman died. He married another woman, and also had a daughter by her. The woman hated her stepdaughter and ill-used her in a thousand ways. As soon as the father was gone, the stepmother abused the girl with words and blows. Then she would push her out of the house, unfed and unclad. In the evening, the father would come home, and say, "O daughter! Why have you such a tired look? Perhaps my new wife does not act quite fair toward you?" "No," the daughter would say, "she does nothing wrong to me."Thus she would refuse to complain. They lived in this way, and the young girl suffered much. At last she could endure it no longer; so when the father came back in the evening, she said, "O father! Take me away! I cannot be here any longer. Take me rather to the Unclean Idol."[33] The father said, "try, my child, if you feel so badly, I will rather stay here and watch over you. Perhaps then life will become more bearable for you." So the next day he did not go hunting, but stayed at home. His wife, however, was so angry with him, that she began to ill-use both him and her stepdaughter. She even beat the latter worse than ever. The old man tried to stop his wife, but she struck him also. Then he said, "O child! You were right, I cannot bear to look upon your distress, and I have no power to help you: rather than have you stay here I will carry you away to the Unclean Idol. He shall eat you all at once, and there will be an end to this sorrow."

In the morning he attached his dogs to his sledge, and said to his daughter, "Now get ready! We will go to the Unclean Idol." His wife was very glad, and helped her stepdaughter get ready to depart. The old man said to the girl, "you must take from the fireplace some ashes and a few coals, and put them into a handkerchief. When you feel hungry, take a kettle and put into it some of these ashes and coals. This will serve you as food." So they went away and drove for a long time.

They came to the house of the Unclean Idol. He was not at home. So the father said, "O child! I will go back and you must stay here and wait for the house master." He went away. The daughter stayed there, full of sorrow. Evening came, and she felt hungry: she took a kettle and put into it some ashes and coals. She put the kettle near the fire. After some time she looked into it, and it was full to the brim of cooked fat and meat. She put the food into a bowl of birch wood, on a shelf she found a horn spoon and went to eat. All at once a board of the flooring was lifted up, and from there appeared a great number of mice and toads, ermines, and all kinds of small vermin. They piped, "we are children of the Unclean Idol. Our father has not come back for several days, and we feel hungry. Give us some food too from your birch bowl with your horn spoon! We know those things very well. They are of our own house." So she fed the whole pack, giving to one a spoonful, and to another half a spoonful, and in the end nothing was left for herself. The vermin had enough, and went back under the flooring, and the girl lay down to sleep quite hungry.

Early in the morning there was heard a great noise and

clatter. The Unclean Idol came flying with his broad paper wings, alighted, and entered the house. "Oh, oh, oh! We heard nothing, we saw nothing, the little Russian bone came to the house of its own free will." All at once a board was lifted, as before, and his vermin children spurted out in all directions; and they piped, "O father! Do not do her any harm! She treated us kindly, and gave us food to eat. You must reward her for this. Otherwise, we might have died of starvation." "Ah!" said the Unclean Idol, "she is clever." He brought a sable overcoat and a bagful of silver money. "This is my present to you. When your father comes again, you may take this and go home with him." He stayed for a while and departed again. In the meantime her father felt very sorry about her, and at last said to himself, "let me go, at least, and have a look at the little bones of my dear daughter." So he set off, and came to that house. The Unclean Idol was not there. He entered the house, and his daughter was sitting there quite ready to depart. She was clad in a sable overcoat and had in her hand a bagful of silver money. She said, "O father! Let us go back to our house!" They set off. The stepmother waited for them at home. Her small bitch, however, also waited near the entrance, and then she began to bark: "Bow-wow! The old man is coming, and he is bringing his daughter and her money is rattling in the bag." The woman struck the dog with a stick, and ordered, "You little fool! You had better say, "the old man is coming and is bringing his daughter, and her bones are rattling in the bag." But the dog was quite firm. She would cease for a little while, but as soon as the woman stepped away, she would bark louder than before: "Bow-wow! The old man is coming; he is bringing his daughter, and her money is rattling in the bag." At last the old man came to the house, and the woman saw the sable coat and the money of her step-daughter. She looked on with much envy, and then said to the old man, "now, you must take my own daughter also, and carry her to the Unclean Idol's house. Let him give her too similar presents." He took the daughter of his second wife and carried her over to the Idol's house. He left her there and returned home. Evening came. She felt hungry: so she put some ashes and coals into the kettle, and put it near the fire. In due time the kettle was full to the brim with cooked fat and meat. As soon as she was about to eat, a board of the flooring was lifted up; and the vermin children of the Unclean Idol appeared from there, more numerous than ever. She grew very angry; and struck at them in all directions. She even broke the legs and arms and backs of several. So they scurried back, piping and crying. In the morning, the Unclean Idol came home. He asked the animals, "well, now, children, and this one, how did she act toward you?" "Ah! She beat us mercilessly. Our legs, arms, and backs are dislocated or broken. All of us are suffering." The Unclean Idol grew angry. He caught the girl and tore her in two. Then he swallowed both parts, and vomited the bones into the corner. After a while her mother said to the old man, "now, go and bring my daughter back. Take care lest you leave behind any of her presents." The old man went to the house of the Unclean Idol who was not at home when he arrived. He opened the entrance, but the girl was not to be seen. Only some bones were heaped in the corner. He looked at them, and recognized them as the remnants of his daughter. So he put them into a bag and started home. Her mother waited on them with great impatience; but the little bitch harked again: "Bow-wow! The old man is coming back, and the girl's bones are rattling in the bag!" "Ah, you little fool! Rather say 'the girl's money is rattling in the bag.'" The old man came. She rushed out and caught the bag. It was filled with bones. "Ah, ah! Where is my little girl?" "I found only her bones, so I brought them home." The woman wailed aloud, but it was too late. The end.

Taken down by Innocent Beresken, a cossack of Kolyma from the words of a Russian Creole woman, Mary Beresken, in the village "Crosses" in the Kolyma country winter of 1895. W. B.

19. Sea-Wanderers.

On the seashore, upon an island, stood a village of the Maritime people. The village was very large, the houses were more numerous than the leaves on a tree. Several people began to talk among themselves. "Let us travel, that we may see all the wonders of the sea!" One of them was "a knowing one." He knew all kinds of incantations, even the chief incantation of the Zyrian people. These Zyrian people were an ancient heathen tribe, who lived on the seashore.[34] All the other travelers were quite common people. They entered a skin boat and started off. After a long time the winds and the currents carried them toward an island. They landed at a safe place and walked along the shore. It was a broad strip of sand, and higher up was a steep bank of firm ground. On it were the houses of people. They climbed the bank, but the houses had disappeared. The entrances were not to be found. Only a number of willow bushes were scattered about and wherever they stepped, or wherever they put their feet a great clamoring of children came up from underground. The whole bank resounded with the noise of their voices. At last they found an entrance among the roots of a willow bush, and entered a house, which lay entirely underground. The people bade them welcome, and gave them food and drink. These people were Polar Fox people. All of them were quite young and strong. Only one was an aged, decrepit old man who could hardly walk about, even with the help of his long staff. The other people soon went out; but the old man stayed behind, and immediately said to the guests, "O you Christians![35] If you are such, indeed, do not stay here for a single night, but rather sail away. While walking above, you trod down ever so many Fox children. If you should stay here for a night, they would certainly kill you out of spite and revenge. Take warning and go away in time!" So they entered their skin boat and sailed away. They moved on for a long time, and at last they saw another island. On that island was a village and some people were living there. In front of the island, in the sea, stood a tree of gigantic size, full of boughs. These boughs and branches were so close to one another, that not even a finger could be thrust in between them; and in the middle of the trunk there was an excrescence, ever so large. They stopped their skin boat and gazed at the new wonder. The tree stood bolt upright; then all at once it bowed down lower and lower, and at last was immersed in the water, boughs, excrescence, and all and vanished from sight. Then they saw on shore a number of people, all one-sided, running to and fro, and catching fish. They were just like ordinary men split in two. The two halves would meet and stick together and would become whole men. Then they would part again, and each half would race along the shore so swiftly that it would out-run a flying bird. These halves of men were catching fish in the following manner. They spread their fingers, ran down into the water and vanished in the sea. After a while they came back on a run and to every finger a fish was hanging. They caught the fish with their fingers. After that the big tree would also emerge from the water, bough after bough, and stand straight up again, as before; but it would be thoroughly white from the mass of fish on it. Every little bough would have a fat fish hanging on it.

The tree stood up and trembled, as if alive; and then all the fish were swung up to the excrescence, when they vanished.

The voyagers gazed upon these wonders, but, being afraid of the one-sided people, they did not land there, but sailed by. After a while they were carried off to still another island. They landed there, and walked along the shore. A village stood there, with numerous houses. They approached, and saw near the village, down the steep bank, a great mass of food lying in heaps higher than a man's stature. It was mostly meat of wild reindeer. The people had neither anus nor urethra. They killed many wild reindeer. Then they cooked the meat in huge iron kettles. When it was done, they put the kettle under their bare armpits and kept it there for a while. They lived on the steam they inhaled through their armpits. After that they would turn the kettles over and throw all the meat down the bank. The voyagers felt very hungry, and wanted to eat of this strange refuse; but all of a sudden there came from the houses men with long staffs, who shouted to them, "Don't touch that meat! It is bad. Rather come here! We will give you good meat, we will feed you with clean provisions. That is offal!" They entered the nearest house. The people of the bland gave them the choicest meat and dried fat and brought in large bladders filled with pure oil. They ate heartily.

An old man was sitting opposite them, and was all the time attentively watching their doings. "Ah!" said he, "so this is your manner of eating! It seems you relish it." The "knowing one," the man with incantations, wanted him to do the same. "Do try and have a morsel!" "I wish I could!" said the old man; "but you see yourself, with your own eyes that we have neither anus nor urethra. What, then, would become of me?" The other one, however, did not desist. "Ah, father! Do take a morsel! I will arrange that you may enjoy it without danger." "Ah!" said the old man, "I have lived long enough; so let me try it once, though I die from it!" He took a small bit and swallowed it. "Ah! It is sweet." He took another piece, and by and by had eaten a large and hearty meal, in the manner of human beings. In due time, however, he felt uncomfortable, and shouted, "My buttocks prick me, my buttocks prick me!" Tears started from his eyes from pain. The man with incantations took a splinter of drift larchwood and made it round and sharp-pointed.

He pronounced several incantations over it, and then thrust it through the old man's breeches, thus making an anus for him. In a similar manner he made for him also a urethra. At the same moment the old man eased himself in both ways, and became like an ordinary man. But the others were without openings, as before.

The next morning, however, the visitors were requested to furnish the whole population with anus and urethra, for which they were paid generously with costly fur. Till then they had traveled among all these wonders and terrors without any provisions, but from here they took along plenty of dried meat.

They sailed on, and reached another island. A single house, quite large, stood on the bank. In it lived an old man and his wife. Before the entrance a big brown bear was tied to a post. It was their watch-dog. Close to the house stood two racks of drying poles filled with human flesh. There were shoulders along with arms and hands in one piece; and the fingers glistened with rings, gold and silver. The heads were ornamented with earrings, and the legs with feet booted in leather and chamois. The travelers were much afraid, but they did not dare to say anything. The old man said to his wife, "bring some cloud-berries for our guests." So she brought a dish full of rosy finger tips of women and children, cut off with great care. These finger tips, indeed, looked like so many berries. The "knowing one" said to his companions, "do not eat this food. Hide it in the bosom of your clothes." They were all clad in fur shirts, and girt around with large girdles of many-colored stuff, as is the custom with our people. So they did as they were told, and after the meal they went out of the house as if to ease themselves. They loosened their girdles, and all these awful finger tips glided down to the ground. They went back. The old woman was already preparing beds for them. "These places are for you, and these also. Lie down and have your rest." They went out again; and the "knowing one" said, "we cannot stay here. The only way to do is the following. We will return, and I shall take my pipe and have a short smoke. That done, I shall knock the glowing ashes out of the bowl. Then all at once I shall howl like a wolf. You must be careful and hold on to me at that very moment. I shall rush out and take you along."

He had a smoke, and knocked the glowing ashes out of

the pipe bowl. Then all at once he howled like a wolf. The bear in front of the door fell down at once and snored loudly. The old man and the old woman within the house fell asleep and slept like logs. The visitors went out and found the skin boat.

They gave up journeying farther, and turned homeward. On the return journey, they made almost no landings, but sailed steadily on. They revisited only those people whose intestines they had provided with openings, and obtained from them more provisions for the last part of their journey.

They were traveling, not for a single year, nor for two years, but for three complete years, of twelve months each. All of them had wives at home, some of whom had been left with child. These women had had time to give birth to their children, and the children were already toddling about and babbling lustily, though not very intelligibly. So they came home. Their wives were told by neighbors, "Come out! Your husbands have come back!" They almost lost their senses for joy, because they had believed that their husbands were dead and gone. As soon as the men came into the house, the women glanced at them and swooned. They remained unconscious for many hours, and could hardly be restored. After that they lived with their husbands exactly as they had in former times. The end.

Told by Innocent Korkin, a Russianized Yukaghir man, in the village of Pokhotsk, in the Kolyma country, summer of 1896.

20. The Tale of La'la.[36]
(Kolyma Version)

La'la was very rich in peltries. Among all the Chukchee people along the border he was known for his costly furs. He was also a great warrior, and lived all by himself; only with his own family. One time the Chukchee said among themselves, "let us go and make war on La'la! We will take his peltries and kill the people." They went, and they were more numerous than mosquitoes, all young men and strong. La'la's father and mother were quite old. He had also a single brother, a mere lad, not yet full grown. This morning La'la walked on snowshoes and broke the one for the right foot. Therefore, after dinner, he went into the woods with his brother to hew out a new board for the broken snowshoe. While he was working the lad climbed a high tree, and was playing among the thin branches near the top. He played there, and looked homeward. From the top of the tree he could see their house and everything around. He played there for some time, and said suddenly, "Khadya[37], there are the Chukchee, coming to attack La'la!" La'la looked up, and asked, "what do you say?" "Ah nothing! I am only playing with twigs." After a while he said again, "Khadya, they are coming to Labia's house." La'la looked up, and asked again, "what do you say?" "Ah, nothing! I am playing with twigs." A third time he said, "Khadya, they are coming!" And indeed, they had come. The old man ran out, and thev followed him around the house. He said, "Khadya, they are going to kill him." Three times they chased him around the house, then one of them seized a piece of a sledge runner of birch-wood and struck the old man on the head. "Khadya," said the young brother, "they have killed the old man. The old man is gone." And after a while, "Khadya, they are breaking down the house and are looting the sledges. They are driving a long needle into mother's tongue and make her drag the tent poles. Now they are gone."

At last La'la had finished his snowshoes, "Let us go home!" They went home. "Why is it so quiet here? Not a voice is to be heard. And where is the old man? Why, the tent cover is torn off the poles! Are they going to move to another place?" Then he looked at the sledges, and they were empty. He came to the entrance. His father lay there in the house, close to the entrance. The old man's head was broken, like an egg. The mother was gone. "Ah, sorrow!" said La'la, "was it of this you spoke of in the tree?" "Just so," answered the lad, "I saw from the tree, how they killed the old man, and looted the sledges, and drove a long needle through the old woman's tongue. Then they made her drag the tent poles." "Ah!" wailed La'la, "what is to be done?" They thought and thought; but the bow and the quiver, the arrow and the spears, everything had been carried off. They were unarmed, and he had only the snowshoes which he had mended in the forest. La'la put on the snowshoes, and they set off. His younger brother followed him. They walked on; then they came to a large lake, round and smooth, just like a frying pan. In the middle of it, on the smooth ice, was pitched the camp of the assaulters. They were distributing the spoils among themselves.

La'la spoke to his younger brother, and said to him, "Listen! I am going to turn you into a fox. After that I shall go straight to them, and you must stay here and wait. I shall go to them and try to get my bow and quiver. You must watch me; and if I succeed in getting them, at that very moment you must appear, and run within shooting distance. Glide in among the sledges, turn in zigzag directions, and try not to be hit." "How shall I do it?" said the young man. "Are you not a Yukaghir?" said La'la. "You must know how to avoid arrows and spears. Run down the lake and lure them on, only mind not to lead them too far away, and I shall follow." He made a circuit around the lake, then he took off his snowshoes and left them behind. He went to the Chukchee camp from the north, along their usual way. He waded in the snow, pretended to stumble, and assumed the air of being very tired. Then he went over the beaten path, and boldly approached the camp. "Here, boys! What about La'la? Have you killed La'la?" "Oh, yes, we killed him with a piece of wood, just like an old woman. He did not lift a hand in his own defence." "Ah, ah! I thought he was a great warrior. I came here from afar merely to have a look at him. I was told several times that people would try to assault him, and he would wind in among the assailers like a wet nettle-cord." "Ah, nonsense! He was an old man. He never struck a blow." "True, he did not, but at least his peltries were numerous." "As to that," said the Chukchee, "there is no mistake about them. The peltries were abundant. We are ever so numerous, and every one of us had a share." After a while he said again, "See here, brothers! They say his bow and quiver are ever so large, as are his snowshoes. Show them to me! I have come from afar in order to have a look at them, because it is said, 'Labia's bow is a three men's bow.' Is it really so heavy and imposing?" They suspected nothing, and so brought forth Labia's arms. Two men were carrying his bow, two others his quiver, and two more his snowshoes. "Ah!" said La'la, "indeed, it is true! They are quite heavy." He took the bow and pretended to drop it. Then he tried the snowshoes and deftly put them on. At that moment, the small fox started off and ran away. All the young people rushed out, and crossed his path, far ahead of him. So the fox returned to the camp, and hid among the lodges. The Chukchee shot at it (as thick as rain fell the arrows), but nobody could so much as graze it. It turned again and ran away up the trail. The young men followed it, shooting and shouting. Two old men were sitting on a pack-sledge looking on at the chase. One said in his mother tongue, "He, he, he! La'la monia'lo khanidula," which means, "Be careful, boys! La'la will tear the stomach out of your bodies."[38] "Why have you given him the bow and the quiver?" His neighbor, however, nudged him with his elbow. "You fool! Hold your tongue!" The young people, however, did not listen to any one, and ran on. La'la followed in the rear, and one by one he killed the Chukchee, beginning with the one running farthest in the rear. He shot and shot. Not a single arrow missed its aim. After that he turned back to the sledges. These two old men were sitting there. He killed one, the one who said, "Be careful, boys!" He struck him on the head with a piece of wood. He took the other one along and married him to his mother. He also turned his brother back into a man. To these three he gave everything he took from the Chukchee.

He went away from there, and arrived at another village. There he married the pretty daughter of the chief. He lived there with his pretty wife. They had two children, a boy and a girl. The children were growing up. The girl already could carry water from the river, and the boy could fetch fuel from the woods. One time the father brought home a large heath cock, and said to his wife, "Cook that heath cock!" She cooked it, and they had a meal. After the meal she carried out the bones and the odd pieces in a large frying-pan, and then she vanished. They waited for her, but she never came back. La'la went out to look for her; but she was nowhere to be seen. There were left only traces in the snow, as if a giant bird had brushed it with its wings. From this he knew that someone with wings had carried her off.

One night passed. In the morning, he said to his children, "I will go and look for your mother. You must stay at home and not show yourselves outside. In three days, I shall come back. Whether I find her or not, I shall come to you." After that he left. On the way, he met a Buzzard. "Here, Buzzard! Have you not seen my wife?" "I will not tell you. Every time you meet me, you shoot at me. Why, then, should I tell you the truth?" After a while he met a Bluejay. "Here Jay! Who carried off my wife?" "I will tell you. When you lived with your wife, you used to bring home all kinds of meat and other food. When I came and pecked at the food, you would not hinder me; so I will tell you the truth. He who carried off your wife is Raven-Son, with beak of iron, and tail of grass. You must go straight ahead in this direction, then you will find him." La'la thanked the Jay and set off. He walked straight ahead, and came to a place where there was a round hole in the ground, just like the furrow of a fox. He looked in. A small old woman, wearing an apron of summer skins, was there, skipping about like a grasshopper. As soon as she saw him, she tore off a narrow shred from her apron, cut it into small pieces, which she put into the kettle. She hung the kettle over the fire; and after a while she took it off and invited La'la to eat, saying, "the meal is ready. Sit down and eat!" He tasted of the food, and it was fat meat of the mountain-sheep cooked with edible roots.

He went on, and after a while he came to another place. Smoke was coming up out of the ground. He looked down the hole. An old woman clad in a coat of autumn skins was skipping about like a jumping hare.

As soon as she saw him, she cut off a narrow piece of her coat, chopped it up fine, and put it into a kettle. She cooked it and invited him to partake of the meal. He ate of the food, and it was fat meat of wild reindeer. When he wanted to go away, the old woman said, "go straight ahead, then you will reach a place where the ground is smooth as ice. There you will see a village. A number of children will be playing near the houses. Many of them will call after you. You must not answer, or go near them. Far off, alone by himself, a small boy will be standing, all covered with scabs. You must go to him. It is your own son." "How can it be my son," shouted La'la. "My son is at home. I left him at home." "You did," said the old woman, "but meanwhile the Raven went back there and carried off your boy. You must wait there till sunset. After sunset, in the pale light of the night, when the moon is rising in the sky. Raven will be asleep. Then three women will come out of his house. They will walk around and cry softly in the moonlight. You must go to them. They are his wives all carried off from their husbands." La'la went on and found the village. In the evening, when the three women appeared, he went to them. They saw him, and cried more bitterly than before. "Oh, cease crying! Better let us talk over what is to be done! Is there any way to kill Raven-Son?" "How can you kill him? His body is iron. Unless, you succeed in setting fire to his house, so that he may burn with the house, being asleep, and unable to wake from fatigue." "All right, let us try it!" They went to fetch fuel, and carried it to the house quite noiselessly, like so many mice, green wood and dry wood, branches and sticks, all kinds of fuel. They surrounded the house with a wall of wood as high as the vent-hole. Then they set fire to it. The whole blazed up, and Raven-Son with it. He had no time to wake up and groaned only once in his sleep. The fire subsided, the coals burned out, and even the ashes grew cold. La'La gathered the ashes and let them fly to the winds. Then he went home, taking along the three women. He kept his own wife and sent the other two away to their former husbands. After some time he gathered all his goods and set off for his own country. The end.

Told by Nicholas Kusakoff, a Russian Creole, in the village of Pokhotsk, the Kolyma country, summer of 1896.

21. The Tale of La'la.
(Anadyr Version) [39]

There were some Chuvantzi people, among them was an old man who had four sons. The middle one was of great strength. His name was La'la. He fought all the time against the Chukchee, and killed a great number of them, hundreds and thousands and more. The Chukchee sought revenge. One time La'la went into the woods to cut down a birch tree which he was going to use for making a new sledge. He took along his youngest brother. The latter climbed to the top of a birch tree and all at once muttered, "Ah! The Chukchee are coming!" La'la asked from beneath, "what are you saying? I cannot hear you." "Oh, nothing. I only said 'Ravens and crows are coming.'" In truth the Chukchee were going to their father's house. After a while, the youngest brother muttered, "Ah! The Chukchee have attacked father and our brothers!" "What are you saying? I cannot hear what you say." "Oh, nothing. I say that some ravens and crows are attacking one another." After a while he muttered, "Ah! They have killed father and our brothers. They have driven off our herd; and mother is following in the rear, dragging the tent poles like a pack-reindeer." "Ah!" said La'la, "let us go home!" "Oh, oh!" answered the brother, "this time you did hear what I said."

They hurried home. Their father and their brothers lay

there murdered. The herd had disappeared; and the ground had been trampled down by the feet of the invaders. "Let us make haste!" said La'La. They hurried along on their snowshoes. After some time they saw the Chukchee caravan. Their old mother, in the very rear, was dragging some heavy tent poles. She looked back and laughed softly. "Ah! Now I am safe." The brothers saw that the Chukchee were stopping for the night. The women scraped the snow from the ground and pitched the tents. The brothers overtook their mother and said to her, "mother, you stay behind here, and we will go on." They approached the Chukchee camp. Then La'la said to his brother, "you also stay here, and I shall go round about until I am in front of them. Then I shall come back to you. And when I make a sign with my first finger, thus, you must turn into a fox, and run about in full view of them. In this manner we shall vanquish them." He made a circuit, and boldly went straight to the Chukchee camp. "Who are you?" "I live farther away than you. I came too late. I wanted, though to kill La'la." One man retorted, "La'la has been killed." Another contradicted, "no, he has not been killed." An old man said, "I am not sure. His weapons though, have been taken, his bow, quiver, and arrows." "Show them to me!" said La'la. It took six men to bring the bow, so heavy was it, and eight men to bring the quiver. "Ah! Here they are! He took the bow and tried to string it, and then he let it go. "It is too strong. I cannot string it." All at once he interrupted himself, and pointed at something far ahead. "Look there! What is that there?" It was his younger brother, who had turned into a fox, and was running about in full view of them. All the Chukchee looked at the fox, and forgot everything else. Then La'la seized the bow and shot them. In three hours he had killed five hundred people. Only a few were left. Then he laughed aloud, and said, "Ah! That is enough; but another time do not come here with such evil plans." The others, who were glad to be spared, immediately broke camp and drove away.

La'la went to his mother, and said, "O mother! Now that our brothers are dead, how shall we live? I think I must look for a wife. You are too old. So I am going. Please get an overcoat ready for me of the worst shreds of skin. I want it for my journey." He put on his best suit of clothes, trousers of white reindeer legskins, and a coat of spotted fawnskin, all embroidered around the skirts, and over all this he donned a poor and shabby overcoat made of shreds of skin. He went along on his snow-shoes, and came to a river. There was a village there of thirty houses. Near a water-hole he saw a number of women and girls. He went there and lay down close to the water-hole. When the women saw him, they laughed and scoffed at him. "What do you want, you shabby one, you dog of the springtime?" They spat at him, kicked him with their boots, and even poured water over him. Finally, three sisters came there too. The two elder ones also laughed at him, but the youngest did not laugh. They wanted her to ill-use him, but she would not do so. "Ah, ah!" scoffed the others, "it seems that you like him! Perhaps you will marry him." At last they filled their pails and went away. "Who are you?" asked the girl, "and why are you lying here? Better get up and come to our house!" "And how can I find your house? I do not know the way." "Our house is the one farthest away, it stands by itself. It is the highest of all, and its skin cover is dazzling white. My father is the chief of the village. He is the strongest man, and the best hunter. If you want to do so, you may follow me." She went off, and he followed her. They came to the house. Her father said, "who is it, so poorly clad, that you bring with you here?" "He is to be my husband."

"Ah! If he is to be your husband, bid him welcome." She made him sit down, and brought reindeer fat and dried tongues. They ate heartily. After that she arranged the bed, and they lay down. He married her.

Told by Mary Alin, a Russianized Chuvantzi woman, and noted down by Mrs. Sophie Bogoras, in the village of Markovo, the Anadyr country, summer of 1900.

22. The Woman's Head.

There was a village on the seashore which had ten or fifteen houses. One of the inhabitants had a lazy son. The father could not induce him to bring water from the river or to fetch fuel from the woods. All he did was to walk along the seashore, singing songs. There was no end of his songs. One day he left the village, and walked so far that he lost sight of the houses. He strolled on, singing lustily. All of a sudden, he saw a canoe of iron moving across the sea directly towards him. He stopped and waited for it. A young, pretty girl was seated in the canoe. She had in her hands a large double paddle, also of iron, but she did not paddle at all. Nevertheless, the canoe moved on, cutting the water like a living thing. It came to the shore. The girl extended the iron blade toward the man, and said to him, "here, young man! Put your pretty head upon the iron blade. I want to louse you with my gentle fingers." "No," said he, "I have no lice, and so I do not want to do as you request." "Ah! At least lay your pretty cheek upon this iron blade. I want to admire your gentle beauty." He felt flattered, and stooped down toward the iron blade. All at once his face stuck firmly to the iron. She drew the paddle back, and pulled him down along with it into the canoe. Immediately the canoe moved off across the sea, going back the way it had come. He prayed to the girl, "Oh, please, let me go! I want to go back to my father and mother, or at least to bid them farewell." "No," said the girl, "I shall not let you go. In former times, whenever your parents sent you for water and for wood, or tried to urge you to go hunting, you were too indolent to follow their advice: now I shall hunt for you and fetch everything. You shall stay at home and be my husband." He cried aloud, and asked her to let him go; but she refused. They crossed the sea and went to another country. They arrived at a large house on the shore. It had three sets of drying poles, all well filled with human flesh, heads, and whole arms with heads, and legs with feet. He cried still louder than before, and refused to enter. She called to him; but he went away along the seashore, down the village, from house to house. The last house of all was small, a mere hut. A small old man lived in it, quite lean and bowed down. His head was white, like that of a polar hare. The old man addressed him, and said, "O, young man! Are you also a human being, as I am? If you are, why did you come here? The people who live here are man-eaters. They feed on human flesh, and they even tried to induce me to do the same; but I refused. Therefore I am so lean, that they will not even eat me." The old man continued, "this young woman is the worst of all. She feeds on her husbands after their bridal night. Bear this in mind: after supper you will go to sleep and she will try to induce you to lie down next to the wall, while she herself will take her place on the outer side. You must be firm and take the place on the outer side. Even though she should ask you with fair words, and abuse you with bad words, and push you and crawl over you, be firm and hold your place! If you succeed in keeping it, you will live; if not, you will perish, and I shall perish along with you. Then you will copulate. She will try to tire you out and put you to sleep; but you must be stronger than she, and tire her, in your turn, and make her sleep. Then you will know what to do to her. Now go home! It is growing late. She is looking for you, and she may come here also. Rather go of your own will. She will give you human flesh to eat. Be sure not to swallow even a single morsel. Try to hide the meat in your clothes or on your body. Otherwise you will also turn into a man-eater, and will never get back to your native place."

The young man went back to the house of his cannibal bride. She cooked plenty of fat human meat, and gave some to her father and mother to eat. Then she invited her husband to sit down to the meal. He took one morsel after another; but he ate none, and hid every one of them in the bosom of his coat. After the meal they prepared to lie down. Then began their struggle for places. Neither wanted to lie nearest the wall. They crept over each other; the girl scratched him in doing so, and he paid her in kisses. Still each time he returned to the outer side. At last she was conquered by his kisses, and let him stay. After that they copulated; and he proved so strong and untiring that he exhausted all her strength and made her sleep. As soon as she began to snore, he lifted his head and groped gently in the darkness beneath the pillow. He found just beneath the pillow, at the outer side, which the woman wanted for herself, two iron instruments, a long awl and a very sharp and narrow knife. She used these to kill the men in their sleep. He took both, and pointed the knife straight at her heart, and the awl at her anus. Then he exclaimed, "iron to iron," and both entered and met within her body. Iron scratched iron. The woman died instantly. He cut off her head, took a long narrow bag filled with odd shreds of skins and pieces of clothing, put this bag under the coverlet, and then placed the head on it. He tucked the cover in all around; then he made a fire, and cooked the flesh of the woman for the breakfast meal. When it was done, he cut it up carefully and laid it in a dish in good order. He skimmed off the fat from the soup, and put it in a cup close to the dish. This breakfast he carried off to the sleeping room of the old people. Then he crept out, and hurried to the shore. There on the sand lay two canoes, one of iron, and the other of wood. He took the iron awl and pierced the wooden canoe in twenty places. Then he called the old man who had given him advice, and bade him go aboard the iron canoe. He himself followed, and said to the iron canoe, "O, canoe of iron! Go to the place from which you brought us!" And the canoe rushed across the sea, going to the shore inhabited by human kind.

The old people heard him get up and work; but they thought it was their daughter, because she was wont to kill her husbands in the night time and to cook their flesh in the morning for breakfast, so they dozed again most quietly. Finally, when they awoke, they saw their breakfast close by, quite ready and waiting for them. "Ah, ah!" said the old woman, "our gentle child has made everything ready, but where is she? Why does she not come to eat with us? Go, man, and look into her sleeping room." He looked there and came back. "She is sleeping," said he. "The night must have been quite tiresome." So they took their meal. The old woman took one morsel, but she could not swallow it. "Ah, old man! I cannot eat alone. It is perhaps because our daughter does not eat with us. I am sure she is hungry. Please go and waken her! Let her eat, and then go to sleep again!" So he went once more to the sleeping room and to their daughter's bed. "Get up, child!" said he merrily and tugged at the coverlet. The head fell off the bed and rolled to the door.

It opened the door and rolled down the slope toward the sea. It rushed into the sea and rolled on over the billows in pursuit of the fugitives. The old people also hurried down to the sea. "Ah!" they shouted, "where is he? We will catch him, and swallow him alive." But the iron canoe was gone, so they took the wooden one and set off in it. After a while it filled with water. "Why," said the old man, "you old one! Cease passing water!" "No," said his wife, "it be you who are passing water." They quarrelled for some time and then sank to the bottom of the sea.

The two fugitives arrived safely at their own place. The woman's head followed behind; but, on coming to the shore it turned into a big round boulder, which is there even now, and be called "Woman's Head."[40] The canoe broke there; turned to stone. The double paddle broken in two.

Whoever passes by must give a sacrifice to the owner of the place, then he will be successful in love, but not matrimonial. The end.

Told by Nicholas Rupatcheff, a Russianized Yukaghir man, in the village of Sukhamoye, the Kolyma country, winter of 1896.

23. The Big Pike.

They say, in the district of Shigansk, near the Lena River, there is a lake. In that lake are some monstrous pikes, such as are able to swallow a man or even a reindeer. One time a big elk went there to drink, and the pike caught him by the muzzle. They fought, but neither was the elk able to drag the pike out of the water, nor did the pike succeed in drawing in the elk. So they both perished. Their bones were found in the shallow water. The cheek bones of the pike were used for a small hut which gave shelter to one man.

One time a chief officer of the country ordered a large iron hook to be hammered out. He baited the hook with elk brisket, and tied it to a strong cord plaited of three lines of tough elkhide and let it down into the lake under the ice. After a week, they went back to the lake and found that the pike had been caught. It was so heavy, that ten men could hardly pull it up. The strands of the cord snapped, until only one remained. They attached a team of twelve dogs to the line and continued to pull. The head of the pike came up to the ice; but the ice hole was too small, though they worked upon it for two days. The head butted against the ice, and the last line snapped and the pike was lost.

Another time they caught a pike, and found in the stomach fragments of a canoe which it must have swallowed together with the paddle.

A man traveled in a canoe on this lake. One time he cast his nets, and waited near them for a very long time. Then he looked down under water and he saw a big round eye, to the left of his canoe. He looked into the water to the right, and saw another eye, like the first one. They were the eyes of the big Pike. The distance between the eyes was about the length of the double paddle of the canoe. He was so badly frightened, that he paddled off, leaving behind him his fish nets; but the giant fish remained motionless, just as pikes are accustomed to do. The man came to the shore and brought a sacrifice to the whole family of pikes. After that he refused to eat of the flesh of pike, and so he was nicknamed Pike John. His descendants are still living. Their family name is Pike.

Told by Nicholas Kusakoff, a Russian Creole, in the village of Pokhotsk, Kolyma country, summer of 1896.

24. Story of the Fish-Woman.[41]

There was a man who lived alone and was poor and destitute. He had no fish nets, nor even a single fish hook. So he went to the merchants, asking for a hook. The first and the second merchant gruffly refused him. A third one gave him an old hook, without point. He took it and prepared a long fishing-rod for it. Armed with this, he went every day to the sea to angle. He was fishing the whole day long, and caught nothing. The next day likewise he caught nothing. The third day he cast his fishing rod, and could not pull back the line, it was so heavy. "Ah!" thought he, "it must be some large fish." He pulled at it with all his might, and at last he brought it to Sherkala, the fish-girl. "What is it?" said he to himself. "Is it my good luck, or is it my bad luck?" He was ready to throw her back into the water; but then he bethought himself, and said, "I am very poor. I can lose nothing by it, let me take her home!" He took Sherkala home and laid her down in the corner of his house. The next morning he went fishing again. He caught nothing at all; but when he came home, his house looked quite festive. Everything was well cleaned and in good order; a good meal stood ready on the table; but nobody was there, and the Sherkala-Fish lay in the corner just as before. From that time on everything continued in that manner. He caught no fish; but somebody kept the house in good order, and cooked excellent meals of nothing. When he stayed at home, the dinner would not appear, so that he was obliged to go out every morning. One day he pretended to depart; but, instead of going away, he lay down on the earth bench close to the window. He lay there very quietly; but after a while he lifted his head and looked through the window. The Sherkala-Fish arose as far as her tail, and then turned into a young pretty girl. She ripped up her own belly and took out fish-roe, which she put into the kettle. Then she swept the floor and put everything in good order. The man suddenly rushed in and caught the fish skin of Sherkala, which lay on the floor. He threw it into the fire, and it was burned. "What have you done," said the girl. "We lived so happily, and now I must go away." She fell down and melted away into sea water. The end.

Told by Innocent Korkin, a Russianized Yukaghir man, in the village of Pokbotsk, the Kolyma country, summer of 1896.

25. Yukaghir Manners.

In former times, the Yukaghir acted in the following manner. When the grave-box of a member of their own kind decayed on account of extreme age, they gathered the dry bones. They prepared a bag of harlot skin, and put the bones into it. That done, they built a small storehouse on wooden supports, in which to keep the bones. The bag of bones served them as a means of divination. In their hunting pursuits they wandered about in various directions. As soon as they were ready to depart, they spoke to the bone charms, "See grandfather! Answer us! How is our present hunting trip going to turn out?" With this they would try to lift the bag. Whenever it felt heavy, it was a sign that the hunt would not be successful. The grandfather advised them not to go. Sometimes it felt so heavy that it was impossible to lift it from the ground. That foreboded misfortune and possible death, and they would stay at home. Another time, on the other hand, the bag would feel lighter than a feather. This foreboded good luck, and they would start off merrily.

The same was done when they wanted to go to Russian settlements for trading purposes. "Eh, grandfather, what is going to happen to us?" Sometimes the signs would urge them on, and at other times it would make them desist. Another day they would be ready to depart; but the "grandfather" would forecast ill luck, so that they would stay at home. After three or four days, they would go to the bag; and the "grandfather" might have changed his mind, and feel quite light when lifted. This meant that the bad influence had passed, and they went forth to resume their enterprise. In due time they would come back from their hunting; then they would visit the "grandfather," taking him the best morsel of meat and fat, marrow and blood soup, also tea and sugar, tobacco, and hard tack. They would put all this into the bag. About midwinter, it might happen that the people would lack tea or tobacco; then they would go to the "grandfather" for a loan from his stores. First of all, they would ask him, "Eh, grandfather, will you let us have a loan from your stores?" and then they would lift the bag. Sometimes it would consent, and feel quite light. Another time it would refuse the loan, and feel heavier than lead. Then they would go back empty-handed.

Every house and family had such a bag as their own protector: They would bring sacrifices to it, and it in turn would defend them and keep them in good condition.

My uncle told me one time how his "grandfather" saved him from an evil spirit; one summer my uncle went in a wooden canoe down the river to inspect his deadfalls. He came to his autumn fishing place, where he had a hut with racks for drying fish. He wanted to get some fishing nets from there. When he was entering the hut, he heard something stir behind him; and on looking back he saw a "fright" [42] coming. He nearly lost his senses. What was to be done? The return was cut off, and there was no chance to run ahead. Moreover, his feet nearly refused to serve him. All at once it came to his mind that his "grandfather's" house was close by. So he rushed to it, climbed the ladder, tore open the door, and fell across the sill. "O granny! Save me!" After that he remembered nothing. He came to himself late in the evening; and, lo, he was lying in the place of the bag of bones, and the "grandfather" lay close to the door and across the sill. The bag had moved the man to its own place, lain down near the entrance, like a sentry. My uncle felt quite uneasy. "Ah, grandfather!" said he, "what is to be done? Shall I go? I am sorely afraid. Please give answer! I will lift you. In case you want me to go, be light like feather down; but in case you want me to stay for safety, please be heavier than cast iron!" He tried to lift it, and it was lighter than a cobweb. "Oh, you permit me to go." He put down the bag, and put it back to its former place. Then he went down to the bank of the river, boarded his canoe, and paddled off. The "fright" never came back. So he reached home without any hindrance.

Told by Nicholas Vostryakoff, a Russianized Yukaghir man, in the village of Omolon, in the Kolyma country, summer of 1900.

26. A Story of Machekur.[43]

Machekur lived with his wife Machekur-woman. Their neighbors were three Mice-Girls. The old man used to pay them frequent visits. Finally, the old woman grew angry, and said, "Cease going there! They will do something unpleasant to you." The old man, however, paid no attention to these warnings. One time the Mice-Girls offered him some fat pudding, made of fish-roe mixed with oil. He ate so much that he could not eat any more, and fell asleep. They took a large bladder and fastened it to the old man's anus. He awoke and went home, and on account of the quantity of oil he had swallowed, he had diarrhoea. So he would sit down and try to defecate; but when he stood up, no faeces were to be seen on the ground. In the meanwhile, after three or four attempts, he felt something heavy attached to his buttocks. He went to his wife, and said, "Machekur-Woman! I tried to defecate, but it seems in vain, for I saw no feces on the ground. Meantime I feel as if my intestines had gone out of my anus." "Sit down!" said the woman. But he remained standing. "Sit down!" she again shouted, and he was much frightened, and flopped down upon a bench. The bladder burst, and the feces flowed around. The end.

Told by Mary Korkin, a Russianized Yukaghir woman, in the village of Pokhotsk, the Kolyma country, summer of 1896.

27. The Mouse and the Snow-Bunting.

There was a Mouse and a Snow-Bunting. Winter came, the coldest season of the year. Mouse gathered plenty of provisions, stacks of roots, and heaps of grain; but Snow-Bunting gathered much less of everything. She found that the snow fell too thick, and the cold came too early. Then Mouse coiled herself up in her warm nest; but Snow-Bunting did not prepare her hut for the winter, and felt cold. Snow-Bunting came to Mouse, and said, "I should like to live with you." "All right!" said Mouse, "then leave your cold hut and come over to my nest!" Snow-Bunting went to live with her.

The next morning Mouse brought a root for her breakfast, Snow-Bunting did the same. At dinner time Mouse brought a few grains and Snow-Bunting did the same.

At supper time Mouse brought a root, Snow-Bunting did the same. Then Mouse said to Snow-Bunting, "why, sister! I have plenty of provisions, and you have much less than I. Moreover, my provisions are of better quality than yours. At present, however, the days are short, let us feed on your provisions! Afterwards, when the days are longer, we will feed on my provisions." Oh, Snow-Bunting was very glad!

"I am willing." She brought her provisions, and continued bringing them morning and evening, until everything was spent. A month passed, then another month. Snow-Bunting said to Mouse, "now, sister, I have nothing more." "All right!" said Mouse. She opened her storehouse. At first she brought the breakfast, then she brought the dinner and also the supper, for Snow-Bunting and for herself. A week passed, and Mouse felt annoyed thinking that she had to share her food with Snow-Bunting. Therefore, the next morning she brought a root for herself, and for Snow-Bunting nothing. About dinner time she brought some seeds for herself, and for Snow-Bunting nothing. Then Snow-Bunting cried from grief. "Why, sister, you are acting unfairly toward me. You eat all by yourself, and give me nothing at all." "Ah, the deuce!" said the Mouse, "I give you lodging, and now I must also feed you! If that is the case, I will drive you out into the cold." Snow-Bunting cried, more grieved than ever, "Ah, sister! Even if you do not give me food, at least do not drive me out from a warm place!" So they continued to live. Mouse continued to eat of her provisions and Snow-Bunting ate nothing, and became very lean, mere bones without flesh, a soul without a body. Perhaps she might have starved to death, had not the month of March come in, as good chance would have it, mild and quiet, and brought unusual warmth, the bright sun shining from a cloudless sky. Some bunches of grass and hillocks became bare of snow; so that Snow-Bunting could go there at mid-day and look for grains left from the preceding year, and peck at the berries safely hidden under the snow. At last summer came. The ice in the rivers broke up and then came all kinds of birds, large and small. The birds alighted on the lakes, rivers and sea. On the shore of a lake, in thick grass, lived a toad, which was a transformed girl, the daughter of a prince, etc.

Told by Nicholas Kusakoff, a Russian Creole, in the village of Pokhotsk, the Kolyma country, summer of 1896.

28. A Christmas Story.[44]

It was in olden times that some girls went to wed the snow.[45] They came to a water-hole, sat down, and traced a magic circle all around themselves upon the snow. They were seated on a bearskin. One of the paws of the skin projected accidentally beyond the circle, but not one of the girls noticed it. All at once the skin under them began to move. The water in the water-hole bubbled as in a kettle, and something made its appearance out of the water. They were horribly frightened and rushed away. Nearest to the river stood the small house of an old woman. She was pious and wealthy. She had among other things a great number of saucepans, large and bright, made of solid copper. She met them in the entrance, and ordered them immediately to put the saucepans on their heads as caps. Then they sat down and waited. After a few moments the door was torn open, and in rushed a large stove, all of black iron, breathing fire from all its openings. All at once all the saucepans were pulled down with great violence. That done, the phantom departed. Most certainly the saucepans had been mistaken by it for the heads of girls, so the girls were saved. That is all.

Told by Mary Dauroff, a Russian Creole woman, in the village of Pokhotsk, summer of 1896.

29. Story of a Foolish Woman.

Once upon a time, there lived a man who had a foolish wife. He beat her and chastized her in every way, but could do nothing with her. One time he said to himself, "Let me test her! Perhaps she will become more sensible." He had some deadfalls in the woods, and some fish nets in the water. He said to her, "Let us go and have a look at them!" They set off. The man examined a deadfall, and found in it a hare; then he found in a fish net a large barbot. He put the barbot into the deadfall, and the hare into the fish net. That done, he called his wife. They came to the deadfall, and she saw the barbot. "Oh, oh!" said the woman, "how is it now? Barbots are caught in deadfalls!" "So they are," answered the man. They came to the fish net, and the hare was caught in its meshes. "And how is this?" said the woman. "Hares are caught in fish nets!" "So they are," answered the man.

They went back to the village, and passed the chief officer's house. Some cows in the stable were lowing loudly. "Who is that crying?" asked the woman. "It is the chief officer," said the man. "His women flog him most mercilessly." "Poor thing!" said the woman, "he cries so vehemently," "Why, he feels pain, therefore he is crying."

They came home and found a treasure of silver money. "Mind," said the man, "do not tell any one about it, lest it should be taken from us." After a while, they had a quarrel. The woman grew angry. She went to the chief officer and told him everything. The chief officer gave immediate orders to bring the man. "Why, you scoundrel! You found a treasure and told me nothing of it." "What treasure?" said the man. "I swear, I found nothing!" "You did, you did!" said the woman. "You are crazy," said the man. "When did I find the treasure." "Ah, when? Just at the time when we caught a barbot in a deadfall and a hare in a net." "What did you say?" asked the chief officer, much astonished. "Yes, yes!" repeated the woman, "at that very time, when the women flogged you in the stable. You cried most vehemently."

The chief officer grew angry and turned her out of the house. Her husband gave her a severe thrashing.

However, she was in no way down-hearted. She ill-used the man worse than ever. "It is because you buy no good clothes for me," repeated the woman, "therefore the people set little value by me, and even turn me out of their houses; and when I pass on the street, no man greets me with as much as a bow." "Why, you thrice fool!" said the man, but she would not stop at all. "To-morrow is a holiday," said she, "buy me a new dress, or I will give you no rest or quiet." "All right!" said the man, "I will buy you a new dress, very costly. You may put it on and go to church." "What dress, what dress?" insisted the woman. "Be quiet!" said the man. "It is too late now. Go to sleep. Early in the morning I shall bring you that precious dress." She went to sleep. The man went to the stable and slaughtered a young bull. He took off the skin in one piece, horns and hoofs, muzzle and tail, and everything withal. This he carried home for his wife. Early in the morning the bells tolled for morning service. The woman jumped up and nudged her husband. "Get up, will you! Where is my new dress?" "I will bring it presently," said the man. "Ah, here it is!"

The woman wanted to strike a fire. "O don't!" said the man, "listen to the bells! You must hurry! Come here! I will help you dress." So he helped her into the bull skin, and then sewed it up. He put the horns and the tail in their proper places. "Now you look quite well," said he. "Be off to church!" She hurried on, like a cow walking on her hind legs. Whoever met her fell down with fright. "Ah," said the woman, "see how they bow to me this time!" She came to the church, and pushed aside all the people with those heavy hoofs. She gored all the ladies, the wife of the priest, and the daughters of the chief officer, and took her place in front of all, close to the priest. All the people looked at her and were much frightened. Women ceased saying their prayers, and clerks and chanters stopped singing. The priest came out and said to them. "What is the matter with you? Why did you stop singing?" Then he saw the woman. "Oh, oh! Is it the Devil. Who is there with horns and tail?" The people meanwhile one by one backed out of the church. The priest took the censer and tried to expel the Devil. He put plenty of incense into the censer and filled the whole church with dense smoke. The woman sneezed violently, and muttered, "Too much honor, too much honor!" Then she left the church and went home. "Ah!" said she, "this time it was just as I wanted it. The people gave me the best place, in front of all; the children on the street fell down before me; and the priest in the church never ceased bowing before me, and he filled the whole church with clouds of incense in my special honor." The husband said, "you are not my wife, you are a cow. Your talk is like the lowing of a cow." He put a halter on her neck and led her into the stable. There he tied her to a post, took the heavy horsewhip that he used on the old bulls and stallions and flogged her with all his might. He cut the bull hide into strips, so severely did he flog her. He chastized her so long that she swooned; then he let up and poured cold water over her head. After that he flogged her again, so that she swooned a second time. At last the whole bullskin fell from her body in mere shreds. "Now you are again a woman!" said the man, and he led her back into the house.

Told by John Sukhomyasoff, a Russian Creole, the clerk of the church in the village of Nishne-Kolymsk, the Kolyma country, summer of 1896.

30. Story of the Forest Demon.[46]

There was a forest-being, a hairy man, who lived in the woods and roamed about the country. He married a Russian girl and had a son by her. The boy grew up and in his turn married and had two children. One time he said to his wife, "my father calls me to his place, but I do not wish to go. Let us rather go away from here." He took a barrel of alcohol (a barrel holding three pails)[47], and they set off. They went throughout the day, and came to a dense forest. He said to his wife, "this evening my elder brother will come to fetch me; but I shall not go. Probably you will hear a noise and clatter in the night time. Be sure to stay in the tent! Not a single look outside, nor the faintest call!" He drank from the barrel as much as one pail, then he went out. The woman remained in the tent, but could not sleep. At midnight she heard much noise and clatter, but she did not dare to look out. In the morning, however, she went out. All the trees around the house had their bark peeled off and their branches were broken off. Her husband was sleeping on the bare ground, very tired. They moved off. In the evening he said to his wife, "this time my eldest brother will come to fetch me. I shall obey him as little as I did the other one. You must keep in the tent and wait until morning." He drank another pailful of alcohol and went out. At midnight she heard louder noises than before, shrill whistling, clapping of heavy blows, and the thud of falling branches. In the morning she went out. All the trees had been cut down to the very roots, and her husband was lying on the ground, half dead and senseless. She nursed him and dressed his wounds, until he came to. The next evening he said, "this time the old one will come; and even if he should murder me, I shall not go with him. Keep this well in mind. If I am killed, do not stay here in the forest; take our children and go away to your own father." He drank the last pail of alcohol and went out. In the middle of the night, the woman heard noise and clatter ten times worse than the two previous nights. Even the tent was torn from its supports and carried away. They fought the whole night long and then throughout the day, and the whole of the following night. This time it was the woman who lay like dead. After sunrise she came to and looked up. Nearby was a big larch tree, as thick as a man can embrace. The old forest-demon wound his son around the tree as he would a strip of leather. In this position he left him dead and disfigured. The woman took her children and went back to her father. The end.

Told by John Sukhomyasoff, a Russian creole, the clerk of the church in the village of Nishne-Kolymsk, the Kolyma country, summer of 1896.

31. Story of Transformed Bears.

Two bears, male and female, swam across a large river. The current was so strong that it caught them and carried them on. The male bear succeeded in getting ashore, but the female was drowned. The male bear waited on shore for the body, and then dragged it up to a safe place. A Christian hunter was wandering about there. In the evening he stopped for the night, made a fire, and prepared some tea. All at once he saw a large male bear coming toward him. He caught up his bow; but in the bright light of the fire he saw that the bear was weeping like a man, so he laid down his bow and waited to see what would happen. The bear lay down near the fire and did not move. Early in the morning, with the first gray light of dawn, the bear arose and approached the man. He tugged at him with his paw, and nudged him, wanting him to get up. Then with his head and muzzle he indicated the direction in which he wanted him to go. The man was afraid, but at last obeyed the bear. They came to the river. The body of the female bear was up on shore, hidden in some moss. The bear pulled it out of the moss up to the middle of the breast, and then looked up at the man. He pushed her right foreleg upward with his muzzle and in every possible way tried to explain his desire. At last the man understood that the bear wanted him to skin this leg. He took off the skin, and on the second finger of the paw, under the skin, was a gold ring with engraved initials on a seal. The bear ordered him to take off the ring and put it on his own finger. After that the bear dug a hole in the ground. It looked like a grave and the man helped him. The two worked together. The man dug with his ax and the bear with his mighty claws. When the grave was ready, the bear brought a number of tree trunks and arranged a framework within the grave. Then he lay down before the man, breast upward. He roared most piteously and stretched out his paws. He wanted the man to kill him and to bury them both in the same grave. He showed likewise with his paws that he wanted to have his breast bared. The man refused at first; but the bear was so insistent, that he gave in and stabbed him with his knife. He ripped up the skin of his breast, and saw a gold crucifix fastened to a thin silver chain, finely wrought. He took this off, and then buried both bears in the same grave. The name of the male bear was engraved on the chain. They were two lovers of the merchant class who used to meet in the form of bears; but one time, for some unknown reason, they were unable to assume human form again. That is all.

Told by John Sukhomyasoff, a Russian Creole, clerk of the church, in the village of Nishne-Kolymsk, the Kolyma country, summer of 1896.

IV.
CHILDREN'S STORIES.

1. Story of an Old Woman and Her Three Daughters. [48]

An old woman had three daughters. One was Stone-Scraper, another was Scraping-Board, and the third was Whetstone. The old woman sent Stone-Scraper to the Bad Merchant. She said, "go to him and ask him for some food." Stone-Scraper said, "I will not go." Stone-Scraper refused to go. The old woman gave her a flogging, and said to Scraping-Board, "go to the Merchant." Scraping-Board said to Stone-Scraper, "let us go together!" They went out, and stood for some time outside. Then they came back. They did not enter the Bad Merchant's house. They said to their mother, "the merchant was not at home." She sent Whetstone, "go to the Merchant, ask him for some food." Whetstone went out, and also stood for some time outside. Then she went back, "why did you come so soon?" cried the mother. "He is not at home." The old woman went herself, and said to the Merchant, "were my girls here, have they lied to me?" He said, "they were not here." She went back and gave them a thrashing. She flogged Whetstone to death, and sent the other back to the Merchant. They went and stood at the door, without speaking. "What do you want?" said the Bad Merchant. "Go away!" So they went. They told their mother, "the Merchant drove us away." She grew angry, ran to the Merchant and reproached him with tears. "Why did you drive away my little girls?" "They had nothing to do here," said the Merchant. "And now I will drive you away too. Be gone!" She went home. There she sat down on her bed and cried bitterly. She cried for a long time, then she jumped up and killed both her daughters. She struck them on the head with a club. After that she sat down again on the bed and cried more bitterly than before. She took her knife and stabbed herself through the heart. That is all.

Told by Annie Shkuleff, a Russian Creole girl aged twelve years, in the village of Pokhotsk, the Kolyma country, winter of 1896.

2. Story of Kundarik.[49]

There lived an old man and an old woman. They had a little son, whose name was Kundarik. One evening they made a fire in the house and noticed that somebody was sitting on the roof, close to the chimney-opening. It was Yaghishna. They were much frightened, but Yaghishna said, "give me your boy, otherwise I shall swallow you." They ran off, leaving the boy who was sitting on the window-sill. Yaghishna called, "Kundar, where are you?" "I am here in the house." She entered the house, but he was not there. "Kundar, where are you?" "I am here, outside the house." She went out, and he was not there. She took the woman's scraper and the whetstone and wanted to kill him with them, but he turned into an ermine and fled. She went in pursuit, and soon overtook him. Then she said, "O my boy! I want to defecate." He answered, "heretofore, when father wanted to defecate, I used to bring from the woods a big elk head, and we would defecate all around it." She said, "All right! Bring it here." He went into the woods and brought back a stump with many roots which were sharp-pointed like so many spikes. "Here it is." She seated herself over the stump; but just then the boy pushed her over so that she fell back and was impaled on one of the roots. Then the boy ran off again, but Yaghishna followed him, stump and all, and, overtook him. Then she said, "I want to sleep." The boy answered, "when father wanted to sleep, he would dig a hole in the ground and sleep in that." "All right! Dig a hole for me." For three days they dug the hole, the boy with his knife, and Yaghishna with her nails. The hole was deep, just like a grave. Yaghishna descended into the hole, and soon was snoring loudly. When she was fast asleep, the boy began to cut down green wood, and he threw it into the hole. In a very short time he had covered Yaghishna quite well, and she could not get out. After that he fled to his father and mother, and they continued to live together. That is all.

Told by Mary Shkuleff, a Russian Creole girl, in the village of Pokhotsk, the Kolyma country, summer of 1895.

3. Story about Yaghishna.

There lived an old man and an old woman. They had a small girl still in her swaddling clothes. They swathed her tightly and put her upon the bed. Then they heard Yaghishna coming. They were frightened, and ran off, leaving the girl behind. Yaghishna came in shuffling over the floor with her bristle-soled frozen boots. She seized the old man and the old woman, but forgot to take the girl. Then she came back and felt with her hands on the bed. She found the girl, put her into the corner behind the chimney, and covered her with a large dish. Yaghishna kindled a large fire, then she put a cast-iron frying-pan upon the fire and said aloud, "O girl! Get up!" And the girl got up. Then she said again, "take off your swaddling clothes." And the girl did so. "Now, come here!" And the girl went to her. She slapped her upon the face, and asked her, "for what did your mother bring you forth?" "She brought me forth to carry water for you." "I am strong enough. I shall carry it myself." She gave her another box on the ear, and asked again, "for what did your mother bring you forth?" "She brought me forth to chop wood for you." "I am strong enough. I shall chop it myself." She gave her another box on the ear, and asked the same question, "for what did your mother bring you forth?" "She brought me forth to make fire for you." "I am strong enough. I shall make it myself."

She put out the fire in the chimney, leaving only one small spark. Then she said, "stay here and watch this spark. If it should go out, I shall tear you in two when I get back home." She prepared to go away, and warned the girl. "Keep house and take good care of everything. You may open and visit all the storehouses. There is only one which you must not open. It is the one tied with a bark thread and sealed with excrement. This store-house is forbidden to you." Yaghishna flew away. The girl thought, "why should I not examine this store-house?" She went straight to it, tore off the bark thread, and broke the excrement seal. The storehouse was filled with charmed reindeer, neither living nor dead. She led all these reindeer out of the storehouse, and tied them one after another to a long heavy line. Then she pulled in one end of the line and threw it across the river. It flew off and carried her along with it. She dragged the reindeer across, and waited for Yaghishna. In the evening Yaghishna came home, and saw the storehouse open and empty. She went to the river, but the girl was on the other side. Yaghishna asked, "you opened my store-house?" "I did," said the girl. "You took my reindeer?" "I did," answered the girl. "You fled across the river?" "I did," still answered the girl. "And how did you do it?" asked Yaghishna eagerly. "I drank up all the water and dried up the river," said the girl. Yaghishna stooped down and drank of the river. She drank and drank, and became full like a water-bag; but the river still flowed on, as before. "I shall cross," said Yaghishna angrily. "Ah! It is too sticky here." Indeed, the river bank was covered with slime. "Say! What did you take hold of when you left this bank?" "I took hold of a tree and then of a bush, and last of all of a small weed," said the girl. Yaghishna caught hold of a weed, and it broke off. She fell into the water, and her belly burst. A stream of water came out of it and carried her off to the middle of the river, and downstream. "Ah, ah! Help me out!" cried Yaghishna. "No, I will not," answered the girl. Then Yaghishna shouted to the girl when passing by;

Take my head for your cup,
Take my fingers for your forks,
Take my joints for your supports,
Take my buttocks for your mortar,
Take my legs for a stone-scraper handle,
Take my backbone for your scraping-board.

Told by Mary Shkuleff, a Russian creole girl, in the village of Pokhotsk, the Kolyma country, summer of 1896.

4. Story of Hungry Children.

There lived an old man and an old woman. They had two sons and two daughters. They sent the younger daughter to get provisions. "Go to the roof and bring the reindeer leg that is there." She brought it. They took off the skin, broke the bone and extracted the marrow. They put it on a plate and ate it. Then the old woman sent the younger son: "go and bring the reindeer tongue that is outside." He brought the tongue. They cut it up small and ate of it. One morsel stuck in the throat of the younger daughter, and she died. The mother cried much. Then she sent the elder boy to get from the roof the remaining food; but he found nothing there, and came back empty-handed. The mother cried more bitterly than ever, "how shall we live now? We have nothing to eat." The old man said, "Do not be afraid! We shall find something. Till now we always have found something." He went into the storehouse and found a piece of bread. He brought this to his wife. She was very glad, and ate it. The children, however, whimpered again, "Mother, we are hungry!" She said, "I have nothing. Go ask your father." They went to their father. "Father we are hungry!"The old man was furious. "I have nothing at all for you! Go away!" The younger boy cried louder than the others, so the father caught him and gave him a flogging. "I have nothing. Go and look in the storehouse!" He took the other boy and gave him a flogging. The old woman seized the oven rake and struck the old man on the back. He fell down and died. The night passed. In the morning the children awoke, but the old woman slept on. They wanted to waken her, but were unable to do so. One of them took up an ax and struck her on the loins. The old woman was cut in two. After that they cried again; but the older boy said, "why do you cry? We did it ourselves, so there is no reason for crying." The younger boy quarrelled with him, until he took him by the neck and thrust him into the oven which was burning brightly. He shut the door, and the younger boy was burned to death. The little sister cried, so he put her too into the burning oven. She tried to creep out, but he struck her on the head. Then he said, "now I am left alone. I will go away from this place." Then he saw a cloud of dust coming down the road. It was Yaghishna. She came to the house and entered it. Then she took that boy by the nape of his neck. With her large knife she struck him on the head.

The head jumped off and rolled away. Yaghishna went home. So they have lived till now, but get nothing good whatever.[50] The end.

Told by Mary Shkuleff, a Russian Creole girl, in the village of Pokhotsk, the Kolyma country, summer of 1895.

5. Story of Five Brothers.[51]

There were five brothers. Two of them were walking about, and saw on the trail some wolf's tracks, quite fresh, but covered with a little snow. They were frightened, and hastened home; but their three brothers were not there. They sat down on the bed and cried bitterly. Then they went out and saw someone coming. It was their eldest brother. They hugged him and kissed him. Then all three fell down senseless. A snowstorm came and covered them up. They almost ceased breathing. The eldest one, however, succeeded in getting up. He crept home, but a blast of wind carried him off to the river. Then he fell down again, and became senseless as before. He was frostbitten all over and as cold as ice. The wind was so strong that it broke the ice on the river. All the ice moved onward down the river, and the eldest brother moved with it. The other two were also there. They were nearly dead. The ice crumbled to pieces. They fell into the water, and were rocked to and fro by the waves and at last carried to the shore. There was a steep bank, where the flow of the water rushed by with great force. They were dragged to the bank, and then under the wall of earth overhanging the water. It fell down on them and nearly buried them. They were carried off however, back to the open water. The river was now free of ice. Two boats were paddling by; and all at once the bow of one of them split and the boat filled with water. The paddlers had to swim for their lives. Everything floated to the surface and the boat sank to the bottom. In ten days the river froze again. The three brothers who had been buried by the fall of earth and carried off by the water were frozen into the ice. They stuck there quite firmly, and stayed there until spring. In the spring the ice began to melt from the heat of the sun. The three brothers melted with it. One of them opened his eyes and looked up. His eyelashes were full of ice. So he died again, worse than ever. That is the end.

Told by Mary Shkuleff, a Russian Creole girl, in the village of Pokhotsk, the Kolyma country, summer of 1895.

6. Story about a Crazy Old Man.[52]

There was an old man and an old woman. The old man was a good hunter: so he filled three large storehouses with the game he killed. One storehouse was full of reindeer and elks, another of seal and walrus, and a third was full of fish. They had plenty to eat. One morning he awoke, and said to his wife, "Listen, old woman! I dreamed last night that we were going to die. If this is so, then there is no need of all these stores of food. I want you to go to the first storehouse and throw all the food out to the ravens and the crows." The old woman refused; but he was so angry that she finally went and did as she was bidden. She worked all day long, and was very tired. Then she went back to the old man. The next day she emptied another storehouse; and the next day she emptied the third one, and threw all the fish back into the water. "Let us swim off," said the old man. The fish, however, was dead and dry, so it could not swim. The following morning they awoke quite early. Neither was dead; and, moreover, both felt very hungry, but all their food was gone. "Ah!" said the old man, "you, old woman, go to the storehouses and look among the rubbish. Perhaps you will find some scraps." The old woman really found some scraps, and brought them home. A few of them were reindeer meat, others were seal blubber, and a third kind were some heads of dried fish. They put all this into a large kettle and prepared a soup. They ate of it. All at once a fly settled on the brim of the kettle. Oh! Both felt alarmed. The old woman seized her culver-tail, and the old man a hatchet, and both attacked that nasty fly. The old woman struck at it with the culver-tail, and overthrew the kettle. The old man threw his hatchet at it, but the hatchet hit the old woman and broke her head. She fell down dead. The old man ate the remainder of the soup, and a fish bone stuck in his throat of which he also died. The end.

Told by Marie Shkuleff, a Russian creole girl, in the village of Pokhotsk, the Kolyma country, summer of 1895.

7. Story about Two Girls.

There were two girls. They had plenty to eat, and knew nothing bad. One time they were walking about, and saw some men on horseback ride by. They went home, and found five men in their house, before the burning fire. "Who are you?" "We are people from the Upper Land. We came from on high, and Yaghishna is also coming. She is not very far off." "Ah! We are afraid. Take us along!" "How can we take you? Our horses are few, and we are too many for them." Indeed, only two horses were tied to the posts opposite the entrance. The girls cried from fright. Meanwhile Yaghishna came. She took both girls and laid them down on the ground. Then she struck them with a big knife; but the knife could not cut them, and not a single wound was inflicted upon either of them. She raised her knife again; but one of the girls snatched it out of her hands, and struck her directly in the heart. She died. The girls started for home. They arrived there and wanted to have some tea. They prepared it, and were going to drink it. The elder sister said, "I am very hungry. Go and look in the storehouse. Perhaps you will find at least a dried fishskin."

Indeed, she found a piece of fishskin, and they ate of it. In the meantime they heard the clattering of hoofs outside. They saw horses that were breathing fire, and that sought revenge for the death of Yaghishna. They struck at the girls with their iron hoofs, and trampled them down; but they could not inflict upon them even the slightest wound. So they went away, all covered with foam and even their breath of fire was extinguished.

The girls wanted to thank God for their salvation. The elder one took a thin wax taper and wanted to light it; but with the taper her own finger flamed up. She was burnt to death, and her sister with her. That is all.

They live and live, and get much that is good. I visited them recently. They washed their house.

Told by Mary Shkuleff, a Russian Creole girl, in the village of Pokhotsk, the Kolyma country, summer of 1895.

8. Story of the Tom-Cat and the Cock.[53]

There lived a Tom-Cat and a Cock. The Tom-Cat went to fetch fuel, and ordered the Cock to bake pancakes. Meanwhile there came a She-Fox and sang:

O Cock, my Cock! Let me in!
We two shall play with little gold rings.

But the Cock refused to let her in. Then she sang again:

O Cock, my Cock! The golden crest,
The battered head, the silken beard,
Permit me at least to warm one single nail.

The Cock felt compassion, and pierced with a needle a little hole in the window-skin. The She-Fox thrust her nail in through the hole, and tore off the window-skin. Then she caught the Cock and carried him off through the window. The Cock sang aloud:

O Cat, my Cat!

The Fox is carrying me off
Beyond the dark forest.
Beyond the high mountains,
Beyond the white rocks.
Beyond the round lakes.

But the cat heard nothing and the Cock cried again:

O Cat, my Cat!
The Fox is carrying me off
Beyond the dark forest,
Beyond the high mountains.
Beyond the white rocks,
Beyond the round lakes.

The Cat heard this time, and chased the Fox. He swung over her head his mighty sword, but she slipped into her furrow and was gone. So the Cock went to market and bought for himself a fine dulcimer. Then he came to the Fox's house, and sang thus:

Jingle, jingle, my fine dulcimer,
My golden one, my sonorous one!
Are you at home, O my red fox!

In your warm nest?

The first daughter of yours is the Small-Stuffed-One,
The second daughter is Palachelka.[54]
The son is Valorous.[55]
He went up the sky
Clap my little staff
At the oaken door-sill.
Bring me, O fox!
An oven-baked cake.

So the Fox said to the Small-Stuffed-One, "go and give him this oven-baked-cake." She went with the cake, but he struck her on the head and killed her.

"He hid the carcass under the sand. And the little skin under a heavy stone, lest the people see anything."

Then he sang again:

Jingle, jingle, my fine dulcimer.
My golden one, my sonorous one!
Are you at home, O fox!
In your warm nest?

You are
Quite fair of face.
But your husband is unfair.
Clap my little staff
Upon the oaken door-sill,
Bring me, O Fox!
An oven-baked-cake.

"Ah!" said the Fox, "go, Palachelka, and give him this oven-baked cake." She went with the cake but he killed her likewise. Then he sang again:

Jingle, jingle, my fine dulcimer.
My golden one, my sonorous one!
Are you at home O fox!
In your warm nest?
You are

Quite fair of face.
But your husband is unfair.
Clap my little staff
Upon the oaken door-sill.
Bring me, O Fox!

An oven-baked-cake.

"Ah!" said the Fox, "go, little Cock, and give him this oven-baked cake!"

The Cock went with the cake, but the Tom-Cat caught the Cock and hurried back to his home. He gave the cock a sound thrashing. Another time, whoever comes, you must not forget to keep the door tightly closed. After that they lived happily.[56]

Told by Mary Shkuleff, a Russian Creole girl, aged fourteen, in the village of Pokhotsk, the Kolyma country, summer of 1895.

9. *Story of Elk's Head.*

There were an old man and an old woman. They had one daughter. They said to her, "go to the roof and bring the elk's head." She brought the elk's head. They chopped it up small and cooked it in a kettle. They ate of it, and in one day they finished it. Then they said again to the girl, "go to the roof and bring the mare's tongue." She brought the tongue. They cut it up small, and then fried it in a frying-pan. Then they wanted to eat of it; but the first morsel stuck in the throat of the girl, and she fell down, with the rattle of death in her throat. The old man and the old woman cried for grief, but the girl soon died. The old woman cried so much, that she brought forth a boy. The old man felt joyful, so he wanted to celebrate the birth. He kindled a large fire, and went to the roof to get a leg of elk; but before he came back, the old woman had died along with the boy. The old man was frantic with grief. He cried at first; then he struck the old woman, and said, "why did the black ruin take you this time? You never even felt slightly indisposed." The old woman was so angry, that she jumped up, struck the old man on the head, and died again. The old man fell down and scattered all around in their ashes. The end. They lived and lived, and live till now, but get nothing good whatever.

Told by Marie Dauroff, a Russian Creole girl, aged fifteen, in the village of Nishne-Kolymsk, the Kolyma country, summer of 1896.

10. Story of a Small Girl.

There was an old man and an old woman. They had no sons or daughters so they prayed to God, and he sent them a son. He grew up quickly, and was useful in their household work. One morning they ordered him to start a fire. He climbed to the roof and pulled the skin stopper out of the chimney. Then he kindled the fire, and it flamed up brightly. He wanted to put the tea-kettle on the burning coals; but the kettle was set awry, and reclined to one side. Some of the scalding water poured out on the boy's hand. He let go of the kettle, and it was nearly overthrown. The father and the mother grew angry and gave him a severe spanking. "In vain was it that we prayed to God for you. Better were it if we had prayed for a little girl." The old woman wanted to put the kettle in order, but she could not even move it from its place. Then the boy put the tea kettle upon the hearth, at a safe distance from the fire. The old woman said again, "bring some wood. We will cook the elk head." He brought the wood and the elk head, and she cooked it; but the head remained tough, however long she cooked it. Meanwhile the old woman did not feel well. She lay down on the bed and brought forth a girl. This girl grew up in a couple of days, and was able to work. The old man said, "Thank God, we have a girl now! She shall work for us and do everything." Again the girl cooked the elk head, and when it was done they ate of it; but the boy had a bone stick in his throat, of which he died. The old man and the old woman cried from grief, and repeated, "Ah, ah! We have a girl now, but the boy is gone." "It was you, old fool! Who complained of the boy," said the old man to his wife. After that he went chopping wood, and in his grief he cut his foot. He came back to the house, and the old woman said, "I always knew you were very clumsy." He grew angry, and struck her neck with his ax. Both fell down and died. The girl also died. The end.

Told by Kitty, called the Lamut girl, a Russian Creole girl, aged twelve, in the village of Nishne-Kolymsk, summer of 1896.

11. Story about Yaghishna.

There was a young girl. She walked about, and saw two boys coming. She shouted to them, "who are you?" "We are your brothers." "And where are you going?" "We are going to your house." She sat down on the ground and sank through it. The brothers came to the house, and cried bitterly. Then they went down the road the girl had descended before them. They came to the girl, and cried again, "why should the earth refuse to carry you? You are probably too clumsy to walk upon it." She felt very angry. Therefore, she jumped up to the earth's surface, and struck both boys on the face. Then she went home. Not a single piece of wood was left there. The two boys, while crying, had burnt up all the fuel, to dry their tears before the fire. She left the house and went away. After a while she met Yaghishna. The she-monster said, "I want to take you for my daughter. Would you like to be my daughter?" "I should like it on one condition." "What is that? Speak!" "On condition that you die very shortly." Yaghishna was very angry, and struck her face. "If I die shortly, I want no daughters." She first slapped her right cheek, and then the left, and flew away snorting with anger. The girl fell down and was scattered about as gravel. After a while Yaghishna came back. She looked for the girl, but she was not to be found. Only some gravel lay scattered all around. "Is it you?" But the gravel was silent. "Who made you fall down?" "The gravel was dumb." That is all.

Told by Annie Korkin, a Russianized Yukaghir girl, aged fourteen, in the village of Pokhotsk, the Kolyma country, summer of 1895.

V.

MARKOVO TALES.

1. Lamut Tale.

There was a Lamut man, who traveled about looking for a wife. One time he found a stone in the likeness of a person. He took it home and put it near the fireplace. He awoke in the morning, and said to the stone, "There, wife, cook some food!" Since the stone never stirred, he got up and cooked the food himself. Then he went off to look for game. He came back in the evening, and said again to the stone, "Wife, cook some food!" But since the stone never stirred, he cooked the food himself. He awoke next morning, and, lo! the stone wife was cooking food. They lived together as husband and wife.

After a while he went to a river and walked along the bank. He felt thirsty; he found a water-hole and stooped down. When about to drink, he saw a girl down below, who was combing her long glossy hair. "Ah, come here! Let us play!" She came out, and they played shooting at each other with bow and arrows. At last he looked up. The sun was already setting. "Ah! It is late. I must go home." He went home, but his wife pouted at him. "Why are you so late? Before this you used to come in time." "I have been tracking a fox." The following morning he arose early and went to the river. The water girl was already down there in the water, combing her hair. "Come along, let us play!" They played again till sunset. When he came home, his wife was very angry. "Why are you so late?" He gave no answer, thinking of the girl, and promising himself, "tomorrow morning I shall get up still earlier." The wife, however, caused a heavy sleep to fall upon him. Early in the morning the stone woman arose. She put on her husband's clothes, took his bow and arrows, and on snowshoes went to the river following her husband's tracks. She came to the water-hole and looked down. The girl was there, combing her hair. "Come along, let us play." "Ah! My heart is in a flurry. I feel as if we had never played before." "Oh, nonsense! Well, at least come up a little! Let me have a look at you." The other one appeared out of the water up to her armpits. Then the stone wife shot at her and pierced her breast with an arrow. Blood spurted from her breast and from her back. The girl dropped back, and the stone woman returned to her home. She put her husband's clothes in their former place, also his bow and snowshoes. Then she removed the sleeping-spell from him. He jumped up, and saw that the sun was already high up in the sky. He took his bow, put on his snowshoes, and hurried to the river. The girl, however, was not to be seen. "Ah!" said he with many lamentations, "she is no more! I do not want to stay here either." He jumped into the water and sank down. His ears rustled, his body tingled all over. Then he found himself in a new world. He found a beaten track, and walked on. After a while he came to a city. All the houses of the city were covered with black calico. Apart from the others stood a little house in which lived a little old woman. He entered. The old woman asked, "where do you come from?" "I am from the other world. What has happened here! Is anybody sick? Why all this black calico?" "Our chief's daughter is sick. Somebody hit her with an arrow." "I want to heal her." The old woman hurried to the chief: "a man has come to our city who offers to heal your daughter." The chief ordered that the visitor be brought in, soon as he entered the house, the girl moaned aloud, "Aah!" He touched the arrow, and in a moment she was dead. Then he asked for some men's clothes. These he put on her body, and on himself he put her clothes. "Well, father and mother, take your last farewell. I will watch the body all by myself." After sunset there came two young birds, two spoonbills. Two high larch trees stood there. The spoonbills alighted on the trees.

O sister! Get up!
Let us play, and let us flutter about!

O sisters! I cannot play,
I cannot flutter.
O sisters! My wings are broken,
My feathers fell down.

O sister! Who broke your wings?
Who plumed your feathers?

O sisters! He who broke them.
He lies down like one dead.[57]

The spoonbills alighted on the ground, and turned into young girls. They came to the one who was dead. The first girl blew upon her, the second girl spat upon her. Then she jumped up, and exclaimed, "Ah, ah, ah! I slept very long! Now I am up again." "Ah! Without our aid, you would have slept forever." They stayed there till the following morning. When the other people awoke, they carried her to her parents. The mother immediately fell in a swoon. She came to herself only in the evening, and they married the girl to the visitor. They lived together. One time he said, "I want to visit my former wife." As soon as the stone wife saw him, she jumped up. "Ah! My husband is coming, my husband is coming!" She whetted her teeth, ready to bite; but the man strung his bow and shot her. She fell back. "Ah! So it is. I wanted to devour you, but you got ahead of me." He built a great fire and burned the woman. Then he went back to the water girl and lived with her.

Told by Anne Sosykin, a Russianized Chuvantzi woman, in the village of Markovo. Recorded by Mrs. Sophie Bogoras, winter of 1900.

2. A Lamut Tale.

There was a Lamut camp. An old Lamut had three daughters, who were not married. Another family made their camp nearby. I do not know whether they were men or spirits. They attacked the Lamut, and killed all of them. The three sisters fled. The strangers dried the flesh of their victims. They split the bones and extracted the marrow. The sisters were very hungry. The oldest one said, "I will go to them. I am very hungry. Perhaps they will not kill me."

They bade her welcome and offered her meat. It seems, they gave her flesh of one of her own people, for she could not eat it. The master of the house was the shaman of the camp. In the evening he said to his wife and the visiting girl, "I will sleep this night with both of you." So they lay down side by side. The shaman copulated first with the one, then with the other. When they lay there tired, the girl asked the mistress, "do you live on the flesh of those Lamut people?" "It is so," she answered. The shaman suddenly jumped up. "Ah! My heart is throbbing. It forbodes something." "What does it forbode?" asked his wife. "Is there anybody stronger than you are?" "Lie down!" said the guest, "since you are my new husband." He lay down. The guest asked again, "Eh, sister, do you ever suffer from any illness?" "Never," answered the mistress. "In the valley down there is a reindeer that belongs to my husband. Its liver is full of reindeer fly maggots. Whoever gets this liver kills all of Us. This is our only fear." "Ah, sister!" answered the guest, "it is time to sleep."

Soon they slept. The Lamut woman crept out of the tent. She took the bow and arrows, put on her snowshoes, and went to look for the reindeer. She saw it in the valley, close to a group of larch trees. It was spotted, and its antlers stood upright. She tried to approach, but it ran away. At last she came within range of it and killed it. Then she opened it and extracted the liver. It was full of maggots. She destroyed these one by one. Soon there was heard a great lamentation from the camp of the invaders. "Arai, arai." She came to the shaman's tent. He jumped up; but when she destroyed the largest maggot, he fell back dead. Then she went to her sisters. "Ah, sisters! I have killed them all." "How is it possible?" said the sisters. "It is not true." "Indeed, let us go and look at them!" They arrived at the camp. All their enemies were stone-dead. They carried out the bodies, and took everything in the camp for themselves. The end.

Told by Anne Sosykin, a Russianized Chuvantzi woman, in the village of Markovo. Recorded by Mrs. Sophie Bogoras, winter of 1900.

3. Yukaghir Tale.

There were two sisters. One time they walked about and met Kosetska.[58] The first sister saw him, and immediately let herself fall down, pretending to be dead. He came to her and investigated the body. He found an aperture in the hind part, and said, "Ah! This is the wound." Then he put his finger into the wound and smelled of it. "Ah!" said he, "bad odor. Probably she was killed long ago." Then he stooped down and smelled of the pretended wound. "Too bad!" said he, "I will not eat of it." The other sister was deaf, and did not hear his words. All at once she looked back and saw the monster. "Ah, ah!" said he, "this is fresh meat. I will cook some of it for today." She retorted, "Better let us go and have a little play! After that you may eat me." They went to a lake which was frozen. "Let us have our play here on the ice." The woman had two round stone scrapers concealed in her bosom. "Here, sister! What shall we play!" asked the monster. The woman put her hand into her bosom and took out one of the scrapers. This she jerked out suddenly, and threw it on the ice. It rolled down with much noise. "Ah sister! You have there some very nice playthings." "You also have similar playthings between your legs. There are two of them. You may tear off one and throw it on the ice." He put his hand between his legs and roared with pain. "Quick!" said the woman, "tear it off and throw it down!" He threw his testicle down on the ice. It made a shuffling noise and stuck to the ice. "Ah, ah!" roared the monster, "now it is your turn!" The woman jumped up and jerked out the other scraper. Doing this, she also roared feigning great suffering. "Go along! It is your turn now!" "Ah, sister! It is too painful." "For shame, I, a woman, can stand as much." He tore off the other testicle, and immediately fell down on the ice. He was dead and the woman ran home. "Ah, ah!" said she to her sister, "I have killed him. We tried a new game, all of my own invention, and I killed Kosetska." The end.

Told by Anne Sosykin, a Russianized Chuvantzi woman, in the village of Markovo. Recorded by Mrs. Sophie Bogoras, winter of 1900.

4. A Markovo Tale II.[59]

There was an old man and an old woman. The old man used to catch hares and bring them to his old woman. She cooked them, and they ate together. One time the old man brought a fat reindeer. The old woman jumped for joy. "Ah, the fat reindeer!" She skinned it and dressed it and chopped it; and then she put some of it into a large kettle, which she hung up over the fire. The meat was nearly done. Then the old man said to himself, "this old woman will consume all my meat. Eh, old woman, fetch some water!" The old woman took a pail and went down to the river. The old man in a moment secured the door on the inside and waited in silence. The old woman came back and could not open the door. "What is the matter with this door?" "Oh, nothing! I have fastened it on this side." "Why did you do so?" "Oh, I was afraid you would eat all my fat meat." The old woman climbed to the roof. "Old man, I put the foot of a hare behind the chimney. Please throw it out to me." He did so. The old woman took the foot and went away. After some time she grew weary and sat down to rest. A magpie was flying by. "O magpie! Please tell me where there are human people." "I will not tell you. When you lived with the old man, each time that I wanted to perch on the fish racks, you would hurl sticks at my head, I will tell you nothing."

The old woman went on and after a while sat down again. A raven was flying by. "O Raven! Please tell me where there are human people." "I will not tell you. When you lived with the old man each time I wanted to perch on the fish racks you would hurl lumps of earth at my head. I will tell you nothing." He flew off, and the old woman went on. After a while she sat down to rest. A snow-bunting flew past. "O, Snow-Bunting! Please do tell me, where there are human people." "I will tell you. When you lived with the old men and whenever I perched upon the fish racks, you would do nothing to me; and when you were dressing fish for drying, you would leave for us some pieces of roe and liver. Follow me, I will show you the way."

The snow-bunting flew away, and the old woman followed. After some time she saw a village. She entered one of the houses. The people bade her welcome, and gave her shelter and food. After the meal they said,

"O old woman! We have prepared a couch for you on which you may sleep." The next morning they gave her a goose, because they had a plentiful supply of wild and tame geese. They also showed her the way. She went on and came to other people. "Old woman, this couch is for you. Go to sleep." She looked around, and saw that these people owned many swans: so she said to them, "please give my goose a place among your swans." Next morning she asked them, "where is my little swan?" "How is that. Did you not have a gosling?" "No, I swear I had a little swan. I call God and the King to witness that I had a young swan." So they gave her a swan. She took it and went on until she came to other people who had plenty of does. "Please put my swan among your does. It wants to be among your does." They put it among the does. The next morning she asked, "where is my doe?" "Why, mother, you had a swan." "No, I swear I had a doe." They gave her a doe and she went out. The next time she slept she stole a sledge and a reindeer-harness. She attached the doe to the sledge, and, seating herself on the sledge, drove on, singing lustily, "On, on, on! Run along the track, harness not mine, on without stopping! Other man's sledge will never break down." An arctic fox jumped up. "Here, granny, take me along on your sledge!" "Sit down, you S…of a B…, your anus on the stanchion!"

She drove on. A wolverene jumped up. "Here, granny, take me along on your sledge!" "Sit down, you S… of a B…, your anus on the stanchion."

They drove on. A bear jumped up. "Here, granny, take me along on your sledge!" "Sit down, you S… of a B…, your anus on the stanchion!" The bear sat down on the sledge and it broke. "Oh, goodness! Go and bring me some wood. I will repair the sledge." The arctic fox went and fetched a rotten log. "That is good for nothing," said the old woman.[60]

The wolverene went and brought a crooked pole. "That is good for nothing," said the old woman. The bear went and fetched a whole tree forked at about the middle. "That is too bad," said the old woman. She went herself, and meanwhile they devoured the doe and ran off. The old woman came back, and there was no doe, nor any of her companions. So she left the sledge and went back to the old man. He had eaten his reindeer, and was catching hares again: he took the old woman back and they lived as before. The end.

Told by Anne Sosykin, a Russianized Chukchee woman, in the village of Markovo. Recorded by Mrs. Sophie Bogoras, winter of 1900.

5. A Markovo Tale.

There was a duck who called herself White-Cap. She asked her grand-daughter to louse her. "O granny! There are no lice on your forehead, but plenty on the back of your head." "Gete, gete!" said the old woman in duck language. "There are none on the back of the head, but quite a good many on the forehead, gete, gete, gete!" "O granny! Why do you talk like that? You never did so before." "Gete, gete, I always talked like the gray geese that pass high above me. They made me lose my wits, Gete, gete, gete!" The girl was frightened and ran away.

For some time she remained alone, then she felt lonely and sat down on a high stone. A snow-bunting perched on a cranberry-bush. The girl asked it, "what do you want?" "Pitititi do you feel warm?" "I do feel warm." "Pitititi, why do you not bathe in the river?" "I am afraid, lest I should drown." "Pitititi, why do you not hold on to a willow." "I am afraid to get a splinter in my palm." "Pitititi, why do you not put on mittens?" "I am afraid, lest they should be torn." "Pitititi, why do you not mend them?" "I am afraid the needle might break." "Pitititi, why do you not sharpen it?" "I am afraid the whetstone might split, and brother would blame me."

"What is your bed?" "A dogskin." "What is your pillow?" "A dog's neck." "What are your spoons?" "Dog's paws." "What are your forks?" "Dog's claws." "What is your kettle?" "A dog skull." "What is your sledge?" "Dog's cheek-bones." "What are your ladles?" "Dog's shoulder blades." "What are your titbits?" "Dog's tongue." "What are your cups?" "Dog's teeth." "And where is your fire?" "A jay passed by and extinguished it." "And where is the jay?" "It flew away to the mountain to peck at the larch gum." The end.

Told by Mary Alin, a Russianized Chuvantzi woman, in the village of Markovo. Recorded by Mrs. Sophie Bogoras, winter of 1900.

6. *A Markovo Tale.*[61]

There were three brothers. One was Grass-Leg, another was Bladder, the third was Little-Finger. One time they ate blood-soup. Little-Finger saw some marrow, and wanted to take it; but he fell into the soup and was drowned. Grass-Leg wanted to help him, but in his hurry broke his leg, seeing which, Bladder laughed till he burst of laughter. Their father went and asked his wife, "where are our children?" She told him. He was so angry that he killed her. The end.

Told by Katherine Alin, a Russianized Chuvantzi girl, twelve years of age, in the village of Markovo. Recorded by Mrs. Sophie Bogoras, winter of 1900.

7. *Sister and Brother Married.*

There was a sister who wanted to marry her brother. One time while the brother was out hunting she sewed a new tent cover and prepared new poles also. Then she dug a long underground passage away from their house, and at the end of it she pitched her new tent. She said to her brother, "a strange woman has come to our camp. You should marry her. After that I will go away." He said, "better stay with us." "No, I will go and look for a husband; but you must go and visit that woman." As soon as he was gone, she changed her clothing, and arranged her hair in a different manner. Then she dived into the underground passage and made off to the new tent. There she sat down and when her brother came in he saw her working on skins. He went back home; but she was there before him, and put on her former dress. She asked him, "did you see her?" "Yes, I saw her. She looks very much like you." "Don't be silly! Women are alike, just like larch-cones; you hesitate too long. Marry her, the sooner the better. I will go and look for a husband."

The following morning he went to the woman's tent, and spent the whole day there. He paid his suit and married her. The sister pretended to go away, but she had gone to the new tent and stayed there. There they lived. In due time she brought forth a boy, who grew up and became able to shoot. His father made a bow and arrows for him. The boy shot at a Snow-Bunting, which grew angry, and said to him, "You good-for-nothing! Do not shoot at me! Better think that you are the child of a brother who married his own sister." The boy went to his mother, and said, "the Snow-Bunting is abusing me. It says that I am the child of a brother who married his own sister." She only said, "Do not say that to your father!" When the man came home, the boy wanted to tell him; but just as he began and said "Father!" his mother gave him a spanking and drove him away. This was repeated several times. Then the father took notice and said, "Wife! Bring me some wild sheep meat." She went to the storehouse. Then the boy began again, "Here, father!" "What is it, child?" "Snow-Bunting said to me that I am the child of a brother who married his own sister." "Ah, ah!" said the father. He took his big ax and ground it well on the whetstone. Then he hung it up just above the entrance. He laid a spell upon it and said to the ax, "if she is really my sister, fall down and split her head."The woman entered smiling; but, as soon as she had shut the door, the ax fell down and split her head. So she died, and he prepared for her funeral. They lived on, he and his boy. The end.

Told by Anne Sosykin, a Russianized Chuvantzi woman, in the

village of Markovo. Recorded by Mrs. Sophie Bogoras, winter of 1900.

8. A Lamut Tale.

There was a man or perhaps a Monster. He prepared a fish trap of willow, and made a weir across the river. He put the fish trap in a suitable place and waited for the catch. After a while he listened, and heard the fish trap whistle. "Eh, fish trap! Are you whistling?" "Yes, I am whistling because the water runs through me." After a while he asked again, "Eh, fish trap! Are you choking now?" "Yes, I am," said the fish trap. So the man drew out the fish trap, and it was full of the choicest fish. He constructed a drying rack, and hung up the fish. Then he asked again, "Eh, fish trap! Are you choking?" Again he pulled out the fish trap, and it was full of the best fish. Thus he worked for nine days. He built nine fish racks and filled every one with the precious fish. Then he built nine storehouses and stored his dried fish in them. After that he began to live on the fish. The first day he consumed one storehouse full. The second day he finished the second storehouse. Thus in nine days he was through with all his stores of dried fish. Then he said, "I have nothing to eat, so I will go and try to find a dwelling."

He walked about, and after a while saw a village. He felt full of joy. "Oh, now I shall have a meal!" Then he sang aloud, "Nia'hu, nia'hu, there live some people! I shall have a meal, and I shall have much joy from it!" Some Lamut boys were kicking a football. A needle case shouted from within a work bag, "Take care! The Monster is coming. Hear him roar!" "What do we hear! It is you that roar." And the Monster sang again, "Nia'hu, nia'hu, there live some people!" They heard his voice, and ran away. Only the needle case was left among the offal. The Monstrous old man came to the village and passed from house to house. Not a soul was there. Only a gray jay was skipping from one drying rack to another. "Here, grandfather! Come play with us! Let us have a skipping-match!" "I cannot skip." He skipped once and once again. The third time he tried he broke one of his legs. He drew out a small knife and cut off his leg. "See here!" said the Monster, "my marrow is quite fat." At that moment the Needle Case jumped up from the heap of offal and sang, "goldid, goldid, nesoyd, koroyd. The monstrous old man has broken his leg! Ub-sub, sub!"[62] "Oh, oh! Stop your shouting! Take this little knife." "I do not want it." "Then take a little marrow of this bone." "I do not eat it, Ub-sub-sub!" As soon as the people heard his voice, they came with knives and axes and attacked the Monster. Some struck him with axes, some cut him with knives. At last they killed him. They turned the body over and examined its back. They found that a long whetstone had entered his anus fully a foot. The end.

Told by Mary Alin, a Russianized Chuvantzi woman, in the village of Markovo. Recorded by Mrs. Sophie Bogoras, winter of 1900.

VI.
ANADYR TALES.

9. A Chuvantzi Tale.

(Anadyr Version).

There was a man, Latka by name, who had an assistant who was called Pondandi. When Latka died, his daughter remained alone with Pondandi. Pondandi worked for her as he used to do for her father. One morning she arose and saw that there was no fire in the house. She walked out, and saw the assistant sitting on the other bank of the river, quite motionless. "Eh, Pondandi, Pondandi, why do you not make a fire? We are cold." He said nothing, but sat as before, looking at her quite steadfastly. So she made the fire herself. "Here, Pondandi, fetch some water!" He did not stir. She went for water herself. "Here, Pondandi, cook some food! We are hungry." He paid no attention. She cooked the brisket of a wild sheep. "O, Pondandi, Pondandi! What do you want?" He did not answer. "Come and have a meal!" He did not stir. She ate all alone, and went to sleep. The next morning she went out of the house. He was sitting on the very same place, looking at her more steadfastly than ever. She herself performed all the household work, and said nothing to him. When all was finished, she called, "Ah, Pondandi, Pondandi! What do you want?" He did not reply. "Perhaps you want a handsome suit of clothes. I will prepare them for you." He sat as before without answering, looking steadfastly at her.

She had a meal and went to sleep. The next morning she looked at the river, and he was sitting there as before. "O Pondandi, Pondandi! What do you want? Perhaps you want to take me for your wife?" He jumped up like a football, and danced about. After one hour he sat down again, and looked at her as steadfastly as before. She said nothing until the next morning. Then she went to the river, and said:

O Pondandi, Pondandi!
If you want to marry me,
Go and kill a big brown bear
For a blanket for me. [63]

He jumped up and danced about, and then started off like an arrow. She said to herself, "Oh, let him go! Perhaps the bear will devour him, and I shall be rid of him." The next morning she went to the river, and Pondandi, was sitting there as before. "Ah!" thought she, "he is still alive."

But when she came back to her house, a big bear's carcass was lying near the entrance.

O, Pondandi, Pondandi!
Go and kill a big elk
For trimming my dress.

He jumped up again and danced off. In due time she went to sleep, saying to herself, "no he is surely dead." She arose in the morning and went to the river. Pondandi was sitting there, but a big elk's carcass lay near the entrance.

O Pondandi, Pondandi!
If you want to marry me,
Go and kill a big mountain-sheep
For our wedding roast.

He jumped up and danced off. She said to herself, "now perhaps he will fall down the cliff and be killed." The next morning she went to the river. Pondandi was sitting there, and a big mountain-sheep carcass was lying near the door.

O Pondandi, Pondandi!
See there the big stone!
Go and bring it here
For our future children to play with.

He jumped up and danced off, "Ah," said she, "now the end is coming. The stone is too heavy. He will desist from his marriage projects."

The next morning she went out of the house; and a big mountain which had stood away back from the river had changed its place, and stood before the entrance.

O Pondandi, Pondandi!
If you want to marry me,
Take a bow with arrows
And shoot an arrow up to the sky,
Then you must follow it,
As swift as your arrow.

He jumped off and caught his bow. He strung it and shot an arrow up to heaven. Then he jumped upward and followed the arrow. She looked up and followed him with her eyes, until he was lost out of sight. She waited and waited, but he did not fall back, and never descended. "Ah," said she, "surely he fell down at some other place. No doubt he is dead." She went to sleep, and in the morning she went again to the river. Nobody was there. "Ah!" sighed she, "it is all over," and went back to the house. At that moment, however, a man came driving a team of reindeer. It was Pondandi. He fell down somewhere among a big herd of reindeer: so he caught a pair of reindeer, and after attaching them to a sledge, he drove off. Now he arose from his sledge. He was quite handsome, and his clothes were fine. He entered the house and sat down on the bed of the girl.

O you visitor!
Do not sit down on my place!
My bridegroom will come,
And he will blame me.

"I am your husband," said Pondandi. "No," said the girl, "you are not. His coat is of the worst kind of skins, and he himself is no more than a snotty youth." "If you do not believe me, come out, and I will prove it to you."

They went out, and he showed her his former clothes and the skin of a snotty youth in the tree. "Look there!" said Pondandi, "down the valley. My father and mother are passing there with a few of their herds." She looked down, and the whole valley was alive with reindeer, bucks and deer, and small fawns. The old people came nearer, and their herd proved much more numerous than the herd of the girl. They joined their herds and lived there. Latka's daughter married Pondandi. The end.

Told by Anne Chain, a Russianized Chuvantzi woman, in the village of Markovo, the Anadyr country, summer of 1896.

11. Lay of Pondandi.
(Kolyma Version)

Pondandi, get up, get up!
Go and kill an elk
For our bedding,
For child's coverlet.
A boat comes from upstream
With such nice girls,

With such long-nosed ones!
I saw the girls
And hid in the cabin.
The girls came there,
They tugged at me,
They pressed me down.

We girls we have come
To cook fat soup for you,
To pick berries for you.
He repulsed the girls,
And hid in the cabin.
The girls wept aloud,
The girls whimpered low,
They were much frightened.
And cursed their luck,
Pondandi drove us off,
Pondandi drove us away.

Told by Helen Dauroff, a Russian Creole woman, in the village of Pokhotsk, winter of 1900.

12. Story about Kundirik.[64]

There was an old man with an old woman. One time they prayed to God, asking Him to give them a child. God granted their prayer, and they had a son. The old woman said, "what name shall we give to the boy?" "Ah!" said the old man, "let us call him Kundirik."

The old man went to hunt wild reindeer. When on the way, a bear attacked him and wanted to kill him. "O grandfather! Spare me!" "Unless you promise to give me your son Kundirik, I shall kill all of you." He promised to give him the boy and the bear let him go. The old woman saw him come covered with blood. "Ah!" cried she, "Pondandi, Pondandi, my husband is bringing reindeer meat!" "Do not make so much noise! It is my own blood. The grandfather wanted to kill me. O wife! He asked for our little Kundirik. Otherwise he said he should come and kill all of us." The old woman cried much, then she prepared some dolls for the boy. She put him on the window sill, and put the dolls by his side. Then they left the house and departed forever. The Bear came, and entered. "Kundirik, where are you?" "I am here, outside, playing with dolls." The Bear went out, "Kundirik, where are you?" "I am here, within, playing with the dolls." He was on the window sill, now within, and now outside. The Bear broke down the wooden wall and seized Kundirik. "When we were travelling, father and I, he used to carry me on his shoulders." So the Bear put the boy on his shoulders and walked along. They came to a big hole in the ground. Two poles of aspen wood were protruding from it, and a sleeping place made of green branches was arranged on them.

"This is our sleeping place," said the boy. "We used to sleep here, father in the hole, and I on the branches." The Bear entered the hole, and immediately went to sleep. The boy gathered a number of heavy stones and brought them all to the edge of the hole. "Bear, Bear! Are you sleeping?" "Yes, I am. And are you?" "I am not. My stomach is aching. I am afraid. I am going to defecate stones." Then he pushed the stones, and they fell down and hit the Bear. He was squeezed down, and his bowels came out of his belly. "Kundirik, Kundirik, help me get out! I will take you to your father and mother." "No, I am afraid you will eat me up." And the Bear died.

Kundirik left him and went away. He saw a house and entered. In this house lived a man and his three daughters. The father awakened the daughters. "Get up, daughters! A stranger has come. Give him food and drink." "Ah! Let him look for it himself!" He refused to do so, but went out of the house and said softly, "Kundirik, Kundirik! Let those girls' buttocks stick firmly to the flooring!" In the morning the girls wanted to get up, but the boards of the flooring were lifted along with them. "Ah!" said the father, "something has happened. Go and fetch my old mother. She will give me counsel." Kundirik went to the old woman, who lived far off, and asked her to come. "Ah!" said the old woman, "you must first help me with my wraps." He wrapped her up. "Now you must help me to my sledge." So he carried her to the sledge. They departed. After a while she said, "Kundirik, Kundirik, now help me defecate." He put her down and took off some of her wraps. "Kundirik, Kundirik, now help me wipe my anus." "There is a horse," said Kundirik, "go to him, he will clean you." She approached the horse. The horse seized her naked buttocks with his teeth and tore her in two. Out of her lacerated anus came a quantity of mice, ermine, spermophile, toads, grubs. Kundirik went to the old man, and said, "the old woman died on the way. She was indeed too old." The old man said to him, "please find help for us if you can!" Kundirik promised to do so. He went out of the house, and called aloud, "Kundirik, Kundirik! Let these girls be detached from the flooring!" He went back and said, "Get up!" and they were free. They gave him the youngest daughter in marriage. He took her along and went home. His father and mother were living in a small hut. A small fire was burning in this house. A small tea kettle was bubbling over the fire. His parents were full of joy, but he only knit his brows and said nothing. The same day he went back to his father-in-law, who was much better off than his own people. He slept there. In the morning he went out and called aloud, "Kundirik, Kundirik! Let my father and mother come over here!" And there they were. After a while his father-in-law also went out and saw the new house. "Ah, ah!" said he, "some new people have come here, together with their house." The end.

Told by Barbara Karyakin, a Russian Creole woman, at Marinsky Post, the Anadyr country, fall of 1900.

13. A Markovo Tale.

The people of a village began to vanish, and nobody knew what happened to them. There was a shaman. He traveled through that country and came to the village. The people were quite sad and sorrowful. "What is the matter with you?" "We do not know. Every night somebody vanished. We have tried to watch, but cannot discover anybody." "Oh, is that so? Let me try to keep watch over you." Evening came, and it was time to go to sleep. The people were hiding in boxes and bags. "Oh, have no fear! I shall keep a vigilant watch over you." He took a sword and waited in the darkness. The people snored soundly, partly freed from their fear. All at once a black dog glided noiselessly in through the window and seized a workman, a fellow-traveler of the shaman. He struck the dog with his sword. The dog had torn off the man's one arm with the shoulder blade, and the shaman cut off the corresponding limb of the dog. In the hurry of the moment, the shaman took the limb of the dog and applied it to the body of the man, and it stuck to his body.

In the morning he saw that the new arm was not the leg of a dog, but a woman's arm, white of skin and with rings on the fingers. "Ah!" said the shaman, "let me try to find that dog." He went out and followed the bloody tracks. They led to the house of the chief of the village close to the church. It was the house of the parish priest. The shaman entered, and saluted the priest with civility. The priest looked sad, "Ah, my friend! Please sit down! I am not able to treat you as is becoming. My wife is sick." "Ah, is that so! And what is the cause of her suffering?" "We do not know. She is alone in her room and does not want us to enter. All we know is that she is not well. Please do help her if you can!" The shaman went to the room of the patient. The entrance was locked; he said nothing and suddenly broke the door and entered.

The woman was lying on the bed well wrapped up in a thick blanket. He pulled that off, and she lay before them quite naked. Her right arm was gone, along with the shoulder blade. Close to her side lay the bloody arm of a man, which would not stick to her body. "Ah, here you are!" said the shaman. "Reverend father, it is your wife who destroyed half of the village. Had it not been for me, she would have taken you also." "Ah, ah!" exclaimed the priest, "mother what is the matter with you. Now, I understand it. She would give me of her enchanted drink, so that I slept throughout the night like one dead, and she would steal away in the darkness." So they took her and tore her in two.

Told by Mary Alin, a Russianized Chuvantzi woman. Recorded by Mrs. Sophie Bogoras, in the village of Markovo, the Anadyr country, in the year of 1900.

14. Story of a Stepmother and her Stepdaughters.

There was an old man and his wife. The old woman died leaving a single daughter. The old man sought another wife, and married a widow, who had a daughter of her own. This widow was a Yahga-Witch. The stepmother had a violent dislike for her stepdaughter. She used to strike her hard and gave her nothing to eat. One day she sent her to the water-hole to wash some old nets. While the girl was washing it the swift current carried it away. She cried bitterly. Then she looked down the water-hole and saw a road. She descended and came to the lower world. She walked and walked, and then saw a horse stable. Several horses stood in it, and the place was quite unclean. So she cleaned it well, plucked some grass from under the snow among the tussocks, and brought it in for fresh litter. Then she continued on her way.

After a while she saw a cow barn. Several cows stood there. The barn was more filthy than the preceding one. She cleaned it well, and brought in some grass for fresh litter. Then she milked the cows and went away. After some time she came to a little house. It was so dirty that the rubbish covered the sill. She entered and cleaned the house. Then she made a fire and sat down on the bed. Sitting thus alone, she cried bitterly. All at once a noise was heard outside, and the shuffling of old feet clad in bristle-soled boots. There entered a small old woman. "Ah, my dear! Whence do you come?" "I have no mother. The Yagha-Witch was very hard on me. She sent me to the water-hole to wash an old net,[65] and the current of water carried it off. So I thought, 'she will surely kill me. I may as well descend to the lower world of my own free will?'" "All right!" said the old woman, "you may pass this night in my house; and in the morning I will give you a net to make good your loss."

In the morning the old woman gave her a net made of pure silver and also a small box with an iron cover. She said to the girl, "give this net to the Yagha-Witch. She will thank you for it ever so much. You must keep the box for yourself. Everytime you feel hungry, you may call your father. Then open that box unseen by your stepmother. The box will give you food and drink." She took the presents and went home. She gave the silver net to the Yagha-Witch. Oh, the witch was so glad! She called her own daughter and gave her a piece of a new net, quite clean and white. Then she said, "go to the water-hole. Perhaps they will give you something too."

The daughter of the Yagha-Witch came to the water-hole. She washed the net. The current carried it off. She looked down the water-hole and saw a road. She followed it and came to the lower world. After some time she saw the horse stable. Several horses stood in it, and the place was unclean. The girl grumbled, "Oh, what a filthy place!" and passed by. Then she saw a cow barn. Several cows stood in it, and the place was dirtier than the preceding one. She passed by with much aversion. After that she came to the little house. It was so full of dirt that the rubbish covered the sill. "Oh, what awful dirt!" said the girl. She entered, however, and she sat on the bed in the cold and among the heap of rubbish, singing lustily. The old woman came in, and asked, "Oh, my dear! Where do you come from?" "My mother sent me to wash a net, and the current carried it away. I looked down the water-hole and saw a road. I followed that road and came here." The old woman gave her a net, the very same she had dropped into the water-hole, and also a large box with a cover of larch wood. She warned her also, "Be sure not to open this box in the presence of anyone! You must open it only when you and your own mother are together." The girl went back and came out of the water place. "Mother," she called to the Yagha-Witch, "I have a box, ever so large." "Do not open it, will you?" said the mother. They took the box and hid beneath a bush. Then she opened the lid. A flame came out and burnt them both. So they were destroyed. The old man and his daughter left that place and departed for the under world. They came to the old woman. The old man married her, and they all three lived together. The end.

Told by Mary Alin, a Russianized Chuvantzi woman, in the village of Markovo, the Anadyr country, winter of 1900.

15. Story of Magus.

There was a man, Magus by name. He had four sons. One of them had legs of grass, another a head of bladder, the third a brisket of leaves, the fourth a voice of hair. Magus said to his sons, "Children! Let us go and hunt elks!" They killed a big elk and carried it home. Magus said to the elder sons, "You, Legs-of-Grass! and you, Head-of-Bladder! Go and bring some water from the river." They went to the river and put the water tub near the water-hole; but they were so slow in filling it with water, that it was frozen to the moist ice. They tugged at it, but could not move it.

Then Legs-of-Grass kicked it with his foot. He broke both of his legs and was dead. Head-of-Bladder was much troubled, and scratched his head. His nails cut through the bladder, and he dropped down dead. The other ones waited and waited, but nobody came: so they went to the river, and found the two dead. "Ah!"

said their father, "let us arrange their funeral! We will cook a funeral meal. Brisket-of-Leaves, go and bring the elk's brisket from the drying-poles." He wanted to take it down, but it slipped from his hands and fell down upon his own brisket and smashed it. He also dropped down dead. "Ah, woe! What is to be done?" "Now, you must go, Voice-of-Hair, and fetch that brisket." Voice-of-Hair brought it and cooked it; but when he was tasting the meat, his throat of hair burst open, and he died. So Magus remained alone.

"Now, I will depart from here. I will go traveling." He walked on for several days and came to Kosetska. The evil spirit was not at home: only his children were there. He killed them all, and cut off their heads. Then he spread a large blanket, and set the heads close to it, in a row. It looked as if they were asleep side by side under the blanket. He also took a large bag and filled it with their meat and bones. He wrapped the bag in his own overcoat, and attached his cap to one end of it. Kosetska went home carrying some human carrion as food for his children. "Ah!" said he, "they waited so long that they have fallen asleep." He made a fire and cooked the meat; but when he tugged at the blanket, the heads rolled off and out of the house. Kosetska was wild with anger. "Who has done this?" He looked about and saw the bag. "Ah! It was you. Magus! It was you!" He rushed at the bag and trampled it down with his heavy feet. All the bones broke, and the blood of the children spurted through the holes. "I have killed you!" shouted the spirit; but from underground a voice answered, "I am here." It was Magus, who had found the under-ground storehouse and entered it, blocking the entrance behind him. "Ah! Where are you?" "I am here." The spirit ran out of the house and back again. The entrance was blocked; but he found a round hole, and tried to squeeze himself through it. His body was tightly wedged in and could move neither forward nor backward. Magus said, "O hole! You are round and tight, turn now into a circular knife and cut Kosetska in halves." And thus it happened. He took everything he found, and went home.

Told by Mary Alin, a Russianized Chuvantzi woman. Recorded by Mrs. Sophie Bogoras in the village of Markovo, the Anadyr country, winter of 1900.

16. Story of Gege-Woman.[66]

There was an old man and his wife. They had three sons. The old man said to his sons, "Listen, my children! Do not climb the roof, do not climb to the upper beam."The next morning the elder son climbed to the roof and mounted the upper beam. He saw from there, on the seashore, that a young woman was catching fish with her own breeches. He descended and went to the shore. Gege-Woman was there catching fish with her breeches. "Ah, you have come!" "Yes, I have." "Do you want to take me for your wife? If so, I will cook some food for you." "All right!" They went home. Gege-Woman cooked some fish, and offered it to her future husband; but he pushed it off, and the fish fell to the ground. "Who wants to eat of your nasty fish, Breeches-Caught?" He left the house; but Gege-Woman followed him, and called aloud, "Gege, wolves, gege, bears, gege, wolverines, poz, poz, poz!" [67] So the wolves, the bears, and the wolverines came and devoured him. The old man had lost the first son.

The second son, mounted the roof, and saw Gege-

Woman catching fish with her breeches. He went the same way, and came to the shore. "O young man! Take me for your wife. If you are willing, I will cook some food for you." "All right!" They went home, and she cooked some fish and offered it to her visitor; but he pushed it off. "Who wants to eat of your nasty fish, Breeches-Caught?" He left the house; but she followed him, and called aloud, "Gege, bears, gege, wolves, gege, wolverines, poz, poz, poz!" Bears, wolves and wolverines came and devoured him. The old man had lost his second son. The third and the youngest son mounted the roof, and saw Gege-Woman.

He went to the seashore. "O young man! Take me for your wife. I will cook some food for you." "All right!" He ate of the food. So they lived together. She forbade the bears and the wolves to devour the young man. Meanwhile the old man built a number of deadfalls and other traps. He caught all the bears and wolves and wolverines one by one. Then he said to his boy, "you may go away. There is nobody left to destroy you." That very night he fled from there. Gege-Woman followed him. He saw a small stream of smoke coming out of the ground, and plunged down. It was the underground house of Haihai-Woman. "Oh, oh! Give me back my husband!" "I will not. He shall be mine." So the two women fought and killed each other. He went out, and fled to his parents' house.

They visited the houses of the dead woman, and took everything there was. So they grew rich. That is all.

Told by Mary Alin, a Russianized Chuvantzi woman. Recorded by Mrs. Sophie Bogoras, in the village of Markovo, the Anadyr country, winter of 1900.

17. Story of Heretics with Iron Teeth.

There were three brothers who were married to three sisters. The oldest brother was married to the eldest sister, the middle brother to the middle sister, and the youngest brother to the youngest sister. When fall came, they set off to examine their deadfalls. Their wives and children stayed alone in their settlement.

The eldest sister had three children, the middle sister, had only one, and the youngest, none at all. One day the middle sister, who had been outside, came back saying, "our husbands are coming home." The other said, "why, it is too early. You are mistaken." She ran out again, and instantly came back: "our husbands are coming home." So the others were quite angry. "Stop talking! Nobody is coming. It is sinful to talk such nonsense." But she would not obey, and repeated the same thing. In the evening, after sunset, they heard the rattling of runners and the yelping of dogs. Sleigh-bells jingled merrily, and voices rang with laughter. Their husbands were coming back from the forest. Oh, they felt quite joyful, and busied themselves getting supper ready. The eldest sister prepared tea for them; the middle sister brought in plenty of meat, and cooked the meal; the youngest sister had nothing particular to do. She looked at them from the sleeping compartment through a chink in the partition. All at once she noticed that the teeth of the men were quite black. She was astonished, and said to the middle sister, "Ah! sister dear, why is it that our husbands have such black teeth?" "Oh, don't!" retorted the other one. "They are our own husbands. What can we say about their teeth. Maybe they have eaten some blackberries in the forest." "It is cold weather now. There are no blackberries." "Perhaps you gave them burnt meat." "It is you who gave them meat, and it was juicy and not burnt." "Or perhaps it is because they have iron teeth." At this time, the teeth of the men were half a foot long. They protruded from their mouths, sharp-edged, and bright like so many daggers. The youngest sister rushed out of the house. "Catch her, catch her!" cried the middle sister, but she was gone. She ran through the dense forest straight on, like a frightened doe; and in the end when she could run no more, she stopped at a small opening and started a fire. She found the stump of a tree that was similar to her in bulk and size. She cut it off and put it near the fire. She took off her clothes and wrapped them around the stump. She also put her cap on it. Then she took a stake as strong as a spear shaft and burnt its point in the fire until it became hard and sharp. With this wooden spear she concealed herself behind a bush. Oh! A noise was heard in the forest, a gnashing of teeth, and cracking of branches, which snapped off and fell down. It was the heretic coming in pursuit of her. He rushed toward the fire, and with his terrible jaws he instantly seized the stump about the middle. His iron teeth stuck in the wood and he could not disengage himself. The woman sprang from the bush and stabbed him from behind with her wooden lance. The burnt point entered his anus and came out at the mouth. He was there like a fish on a roasting rod. She ran the other end of the stake deep into the ground, and left him there. She was afraid to return home, and went to another settlement not far away. When she had told her story the men took their spears and axes and went in search of the monsters. When they came to the house, the heretics had gone. The women and children had also gone. They looked for the bones, supposing that the monsters might have eaten the people, but they found nothing: It is not known what they did to their captives. Perhaps they carried the women away and married them. The real husbands of the women came home after a week, but their house was empty. The end.

Told by Mary Alin, a Russianized Chuvantzi woman. Recorded by Mrs. Sophie Bogoras in the village of Markovo, the Anadyr country, winter of 1900.

18. Story of the Fox and the Wolf.[68]

The man pursued Fox with dogs, but Fox succeeded in plunging into the nest of a polar owl.[70] The man chopped at the trunk with his heavy ax. "O gossip! I want to fly out." "Ah, gossip! Do as if you have too; but before doing so please pass water upon my neck," said the Fox. Owl passed water upon Fox's neck. When the man caught Fox by the neck, she slipped out of his fingers and ran off. The dogs followed her. She ran to and fro, until she was tired. Then she called to Owl, "O gossip! Teach me how to fly." "All right! Sit down on my back!" The owl alighted and carried off Fox. They flew up high into the air. "Oh dear!" said Fox. "I know how to fly, but I do not know how to alight." Owl pretended to throw her down. "O Lord! Let it be upon the moss! O God! let it be upon a soft place!" Owl threw her down and Fox was killed.

Told by Mary Alin, a Russianized Chuvantzi woman. Recorded by Mrs. Sopkie Bogoras in the village of Markovo, the Anadyr country, winter of 1900.

Footnotes:

[1] *These tales were collected among the Tundra Yukaghir on the western tundra of the Kolyma country. The Tundra Yukaghir have a mixture of Tungus blood, and call themselves "Tungus" in the Russian and in the Yakut languages. Though the language of the tales is Yukaghir they were written down mostly without the original text. Conversation with the narrators was carried on in the Chukchee language and partly also in Russian. The tales often include well-known episodes of Old World folklore, borrowed from the Yakut or from Russian neighbors. Most of them had no titles. The titles have been introduced by me according to the contents of the tales.*

[2] *This tale is Tundra Yukaghir, though the hero is called a Lamut. For Masters and Owners, see Bogoras, "The Chukchee" (Publication of the Jesup North Pacific Expedition, vol. 7).*

[3] *This story represents a Tundra Yukaghir version of the well-known tale of the dragon and the young princess.*

[4] *This tale represents a mixture of some Russian and Yakut episodes adapted to the Ideas and customs of the tundra inhabitants. Some details are curious enough; such, for instance, as nails driven into the flesh of the heel, which undoubtedly represent spurs, etc.*

[5] *The Lamut cover their tent with well curried reindeer skin. The Tundra Yukaghir use partly birchbark, partly reindeer skin, clipped short and well smoked, bought chiefly from the Chukchee.*

[6] *These tales were collected among the Lamut living on the upper course of the Omolon River and on its affluents in the Kolyma country, a few also among the Lamut of the Chaun desert met within the Russian village of Nishne-Kolymsk. They were written down without the original texts. The Lamut people living on the river Chaun are a branch of this tribe that has migrated farthest to the northeast. They are composed of stragglers from several clans of the Kolyma country, who came to the Chaun desert for various reasons; therefore, they do not form a separate clan. Their ways of living in the treeless tundra of*

Chaun, however, are different from those of all other Lamut and are nearer to the mode of life of the Chukchee, among whom they dwell. They number about thirty or forty families.

[7] *Among the Tungus and the Lamut, cradles of small children are so constructed that they may form one half of the usual pack load of a pack reindeer so they may be carried along with infants on the reindeer back.*

[8] *The polar wolf is of light gray color, sometimes almost dirty white. The wolverene is brown.*

[9] *One of the usual invocations. "You man!"*

[10] *The Lamut consider themselves, and are considered by the Russians, as the closest allies of the latter in every struggle against other more stubborn and refractory tribes, such as the Chukchee and the Koryak.*

[11] *The type of house generally used among Russian Creoles and Russianized natives, a square log cabin, having a fireplace in the corner, with a straight chimney made of wood and plastered with clay, the so-called "Yakut chimney." It is improbable that this chimney is really a Yakut invention. The ancient type of Yakut house had only an uncovered fireplace, with an opening in the roof above it. At the present time, however, the "Yakut chimney" is used everywhere among*

the Yakut, as well as among Russian Creoles. W. B.

[12] *This passage is interesting, since it shows that perhaps some of the native peoples on the Kolyma River had houses with two entrances, and that some members of the family were not allowed to pass through the main entrance. This recalls the type of house of the Maritime Koryak and Kamchadal, with its different entrances for winter and summer. Among the Koryak, as well as among the Kamchadal, in former times, women and children, also transformed shamans, often entered, even in the winter time, by the rear entrance room, the storage room, while men considered it beneath their dignity to do so (see W. Jochelson, "The Koryak," Publications of the Jellup North Pacific Expedition, vol. VI). It is quite certain that this tale, though it mentions the Tungus, must have referred, not to the nomadic reindeer-riding Tungus, with their light tents of curried reindeer skin, but to the people living more or less sedentary lives along the Kolyma River or on the seacoast near its mouth. On the Bear Islands, for example, were found remnants of some houses, deserted long ago. The people living along the Kolyma were chiefly Yukaghir; and along the seacoast, also the little known Ca'adet and Sholags. At the present time, among the Russian Creoles and the Russianized natives on the Kolyma, several types of houses are in use; but the ancient type of house cannot be ascertained, because of the preponderant influence of the Russian log cabin with its wooden chimney of so-called "Yakut" type. W. B.*

[13] *I give also the Russian words, which are arranged in the form of a lay. The burden is said to be Yukaghir and to have no particular meaning, like so many other burdens. W. B.*

[14] *In Russian, imitative of the sound of the croaking. W. B.*

[15] *Compare various versions of this well-known tale about Raven feigning death: Bogoras "Materials for the Study of the Chukchee Language and Folk-Lore collected in the Kolyma District," W. B.*

[16] *Probably in an earlier version of this story the following words were really told in the Yukaghir language. W. B.*

[17] *Similar tales are met among all the native tribes of these countries. W. B.*

[18] *The Russianized natives of the Kolyma have a very strong superstitious fear of the bear. They never mention its name, but call him "he" or "grandfather." The bear is considered as a mighty shaman, the man of the wood. "He knows everything," say the people. None of them dares to attack a bear, even when the latter comes to the fishing camp and plunders the stores of dried fish and oil. Even the setting of deadfalls for bears is considered by most people as a sin against the bear. It is curious to notice that among the natives (Yukaghir, Tungus, Chukchee) this kind of superstitious fear and worship, though it also exists, is never felt to such an extent as among the Russian Creoles*

and the Russianized natives.W. B.

[19] *These details belong to Old-Russian folklore, and, indeed, are met within the folk stories of various peoples of the Old World.W. B.*

[20] *This tale represents a version of the well-known European story. Several details, however, belong to the native life. The underground oven is a primitive device, although it is not used at present in northeastern Asia, being superceded by the so-called Russian oven, made of bricks or of beaten earth. In more ancient times, the oven dug in the ground may have been used by the natives.W. B.*

[21] *Witch Yagha (literally "old woman Yagha") is a she-monster often Appearing in Old-Russian folk stories. It is presumed that in the Star mythology the witch Yagha was the personification of winter. Yaghishna is, properly speaking, the name of the daughter of Yagha, formed with the Old-Russian suffix ahna or vna. Daughters of Yagha often appear in Russian tales; but their name, Yaghishna, is known only in the Kolyma stories. And, by the way, those stories confuse the mother and her daughters, and call the witch Yagha also Yaghishna. Yagha, Yaghishna of the Russian tales of northeastern Asia, often appears as a being more like the American Snenek than the Old-Russian Yagha (see, for instance, No. 9 of the Markovo tales).W. B.*

[22] *The Russian log cabin and the Yakut hut are surrounded by a low earth wall up to the window-sills. This wall serves also as a bench.*

W. B.

[23] *Small log cabins, or houses of other types, are built in various places for the use of travelers, especially along the trading or official routes. They are called in local Russian "cooking-house." W. B.*

[24] *A kind of soup prepared of bread-crumbs or flour roasted in butter, and then boiled in water. In former times it was generally used in these regions for breakfast or supper. At present brick-tea is substituted for it. W. B.*

[25] *In local Russian it is called "heretic." In colloquial Russian, in Europe and Asia, "heretic" is used as a synonym for "devil" or "evil spirit." W. B.*

[26] *Grave-boxes made of wood were used by the Yukaghir. They are met within the country of the Kolyma, chiefly in deep woods, on the banks of some lonesome little river, as described in the tale. This tale expresses the superstitious fear of the ancient grave-boxes common to all the peoples of the country, the remainder of the Yukaghir included.*

[27] *For the last hundred years, the northern MiatushskI clan has been living on the Great Anui River, in the Lower Kolyma country. This clan has been superficially Russianized. Their way of living is quite Russo-Yukaghir. They have no cattle, and catch their fish not in the*

lakes, but in the Great Anui and Kolyma rivers. W. B.

[28] *This indicates that they were probably Yakut. The tribute chief in local Russian is literally, "head". This chief was elected by several clans related to one another and forming together one tribal branch. W. B.*

[29] *Fits of shamanistic hysteria (see Bogoras, "The Chukchee")- Among the Russian and Russianized natives, both on the Anadyr and the Kolyma, women often have so-called "fits." The patient, during the fit, sings improvised tunes, and even pronounces words of an unknown language. When coming to herself, she pretends not to remember what she has done. Such singing is also called shamanistic and probably all this really represents the remnants of a more ancient shamanistic practice. W. B.*

[30] *This tale seems to be composed of mixed elements, Russian and native. The sables that play so prominent a role in it, were quite abundant in the Kolyma country a century ago, but since the sixties of the nineteenth century, not a single track of a sable has been met with in the Kolyma, partly because they have been mercilessly pursued and partly because they have migrated to the south. W. B.*

[31] *This story refers perhaps to some real incident. Events like this still happen in north-eastern Siberia. However, the manner in which it is told corresponds to the style of local Russian folklore. W. B.*

[32] *This is a version of the well-known Russian tale, but with some details of local life. W. B.*

[33] *"Unclean Idol" is usually applied in Russian stories to representations of heathenism. The word (unclean) is derived from the Latin for "pagan." Here, however, it is simply a monster. W. B.*

[34] *The Zyrian tribe is of Finnish origin. The Zyrians live on both sides of the Northern Ural Mountains along the Pechora River, and also along some tributaries of the Obi River. A confused remembrance of them was brought into northeastern Asia by Russian cossicks and other immigrants, the greater part of whom came from northern European Russia and all along the northern parts of Siberia. W. B.*

[35] *Literally, "orthodox". An invocation much used in Russian among the larger classes of people, meaning about the same as the English "gentlemen." W. B.*

[36] *This story is very interesting, because it treats of La'la, the tribal hero of the Chuvantzi, whose name is known to the present day among the last remnants of this tribe, and also speaks of the wars between the Chuvantzi and the Chukchee. It is probably only a fragment of a longer tale. The episodes composing it reappear in several other tales among the Russianized natives, Chukchee, and Yukaghir. The Kolyma version of this story, however, calls La'la and his brother*

Yukaghir. The interchange of these two tribal names, adds to the probability that the Chuvantzi were a branch of the Yukaghir tribe (see Bogoras, "The Chukchee"). W. B.

[37] *This word was indicated as belonging to the Chuvantzi language. It is supposed to mean "elder brother." W. B.*

[38] *In dressing the hunting-quarry, the belly is ripped up and the stomach and other intestines are immediately pulled out. W. B.*

[39] *Inserted here for the purpose of ready comparison with the preceding tale. W. B.*

[40] *The stone canoe and the woman's head are said to lie on the Arctic shore somewhere near the mouth of the Baranikha River, east of the Kolyma River, in a part of the country at present uninhabited. The natives say that in former times, before the coming of the Russians, a considerable village stood here, but at present there are no visible traces of it. W. B.*

[41] *Compare this very curious fish tale with that of the Koryak (Bogoras, in Jochelson, "The Koryak" (The Jesup North Pacific Expedition, vol. 6), also with Indian tales of a similar character (Bogoras, "The Folklore of Northeastern Asia, as compared with that of Northwestern America," American Anthropologist, Vol. 4, 1902), W. B.*

[42] *In Russian Creole literally, "phantom", or literally, "Aright." Both these words are unknown in European Russian though they are clearly of Russian origin. W. B.*

[43] *This tale represents only one of the well-known episodes of the story of Raven and the Mice. I give it here because of the names Machekur and Machekiu'-Woman, which have replaced the usual Kutq (Ku'rgil) and Miti. Perhaps these names belong to some Yukaghir version of the story. W. B.*

[44] *This pretty tale is used as a kind of introduction to the well-known story of a young prince who married the transformed Toad-Girl. I omit the story itself, however, which treats throughout of princes and princesses, and has nothing whatever to do with the life of northeastern Asia. W. B.*

[45] *It is a kind of old Russian divination, practised on Christmas Eve or Twelfth Night. Young girls "wed the snow" and, according to the marks left on the snow by their fingers, foretell the future chiefly in reference to their possible marriage during the coming year. W. B.*

[46] *In Russian meaning also the master of the forest. (see Bogoras, "The Chukchee." W. B.*

[47] *A Russian "pail" is equal to 2.70 gallons. A barrel of three pails forms one side-pack of the usual load of the pack horse. W. B.*

[48] *The children of Russian Creoles and Russianized natives (chiefly girls) in the Kolyma country have their own stories, which they relate to one another. These stories are mostly simple, short, full of reiteration. They consist partly of the usual folk-tale material, and partly of the details of real life. The latter is the case with this story. It is sad to think that young girls should compose stories exhibiting such response to the circumstances of life of the lower people in the Kolyma country, of Russians as well as Russianized natives. On the other hand, it is possible that all these incidents of hungry children choked to death by the first morsel swallowed, old men and old women dying or killing each other, etc., represent elements of a cycle of stories more ancient than the advent of the Russian, and belonging to the Yukaghir inhabitants of the country. W. B.*

[49] *Kundarik or Eundirik (in the Anadyr), a small bird (Acanthis exilipea). W. B.*

[50] *One of the usual final refrains of the Russian folk-stories. The most frequently used are: "they live and live and get much of the good." "They lived and lived, and live till now." But in northeastern Asia, with the ill-starred Creoles, the first refrain changed to a negative: "they live and live, and get nothing good whatever." W. B.*

[51] *I am not sure that this story belongs to the children's cycle. It looks much more like some mutilated version of a longer story of consider-*

able interest. To my regret, however, I could find no other version of it. W. B.

[52] *This story is based on one of the episodes of the well-known story of the Raven Kutq. W. B.*

[53] *Among the Russians of Europe several versions of it are known, mostly in rhymed prose. The Kolyma version is also in rhymed prose; but its form seems to be more ancient, and some of its details are not without interest. W. B.*

[54] *The meaning of this name is unknown. Both names are of local, probably Yukaghir, provenience. W. B.*

[55] *This and the following line are probably inserted from an ancient conundrum: "The mother is thick, the daughter is red, the son is valorous, went up the sky. Oven, fire, smoke." W.B.*

[56] *According to another version, likewise from the Kolyma, the Tom-Cat killed also the mother Fox. He found the Cock firmly frozen in a block of ice lying in the corner. He broke the ice, and thawed the Cock's body before the fire. The Cock came to life, and crowed lustily. W. B.*

[57] *In Russian this is a kind of rhymed prose.*

[58] *The narrator said that this was a Yukaghir "bad spirit." She knew nothing more about this spirit. W. B.*

[59] *This tale like some others, was indicated as a real Markovo tale, in contrast to others which were indicated as Lamut, Yukahgir, or Chuvantzi tales, or again, as Russian tales coming from Russia. It represents, however, a mixture of elements, Russian and native. W. B.*

[60] *In Russian all this is rhymed prose, though this rhymed version is somewhat different from the usual rhymed versions of the latter half of this tale as known in European Russia. W. B.*

[61] *This tale is met with in European Russia in several versions. Some details, however, for instance, blood-soup with marrow in it, belong to northeastern Asia. W. B.*

[62] *These words represent probably an imitation of Lamut talk, though they have no particular meaning. The last word is in the Russian-Chukchee-Lamut trading Jargon, and means "food," to "eat."*

[63] *This tale is probably of Chuvantzi provenience. It is remarkable for the fact that some fragments of verse have been arranged in the form of an old Russian lay, although the life it describes is of native color. In the Kolyma country this tale has been transformed into a similar lay, more coherent in character, used chiefly as a lullaby. W. B.*

[64] *These words were indicated as belonging to the Chuvantzi language.W. B.*

[65] *Old nets are used in the households of the Russian and the Russianized natives instead of towels and napkins. W. B.*

[66] *In Russian, probably meaning "woman who cried "gege, gege." W. B.*

[67] *One of the calls addressed to the dog-team (see Bogoras, "The Chukchee").*

[68] *This is the usual OldWorld story telling how Fox pretended to fish through a hole in the ice, and then tempted Wolf to do the same: wolf lost his tail in the ice. Fox feigned death, and was picked up by a passing farmer, etc. I give here only an episode which seems of local character.W. B.*

[69] *Some of the nests of these large owls are said to be placed within hollow trunks of trees, or among piles of driftwood which are found at certain places all along the arctic coast. (see Bogoras, "The Chukchee.") W. B.*